# Kiskadee Girl

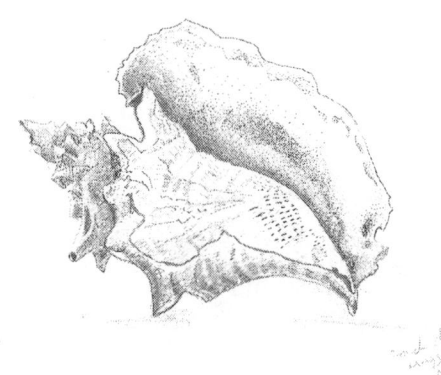

*Maggie Harris*

Kingston University Press Ltd,
Kingston University
Penrhyn Road,
Kingston-upon-Thames,
Surrey KT1 2EE

Contents © Maggie Harris 2011

The right of the above author to be identified as the author of this work has been asserted in accordance with the Copyright, Designs and Patent Act 1988.

British Library Cataloguing in Publication Data available.

ISBN 978-1-899999-50-7

Set in Palatino
Typeset by: Peter Kenyon
Image Layout by: Peter Kenyon

Printed in the UK by Lightning Source
Cover by Gudrun Jobst www.yotedesign.com

All rights reserved. No part of this publication may be Reproduced, stored in or introduced into a retrieval system, or transmitted, in any form, or by any means electronic, mechanical, photocopying, recording or otherwise, without the prior permission of the publisher. Any person who commits any unauthorised act in relation to this publication may be liable to criminal prosecution and civil claims for damages.

*In honour of those who have gone before*

## About the author

Maggie Harris lectures on international writing in schools and at Southampton University. In 2008 she was a winner in the prestigious KUP life-writing prize and her previous publications include *Limbolands* (Mango Publishing), which won the Guyana Prize for Literature 2000. She edited *Sixty Poems for Haiti* (Cane Arrow Press) and her poems and short stories have appeared in journals such as *Poetry Wales*, *Wasafiri* and *Agenda*, and in anthologies published by Virago and LittleBrown.

The author would like to acknowledge Arts Council South-East, who granted a New Writing bursary so this memoir could be written.

- Author Maggie Harris on her father's shoulders

# Kiskadee Girl

## Maggie Harris

Prologue .... 6
The Conch Shell .... 11
Wheeling .... 12
All colours under the sun .... 24
Me .... 37
Early years .... 52
Lucille .... 65
Sisters .... 70
New Amsterdam Story .... 77
Rum and Coca-Cola .... 97
Corentyne Tales (1) .... 108
Schooldays, early .... 113
Passing .... 120
Corentyne Tales (2) .... 129
Kwakwani .... 134
St Rose's .... 142
Boys, boys, boys .... 156
Daddy .... 167
Hot Lime .... 175
Love, love .... 187
Girls go wild in Georgetown .... 203
Verandas .... 209
Where poems came .... 213

# Prologue

*1971*

So this was it. A country from an aeroplane window.

All those months of planning culminated in a gathering at Timehri Airport. Family groups cluster in the departure lounge. Bags and grips wait by new shoes. Handbags laden with passport, tickets, letters, addresses. Mothers cry, uncles fetch drinks, running children divert attention from the emotion of the moment. You, embarrassed by the whole shenanigans. You didn't want to come, you told me.

Last night, all I could think of was how much I wanted you to make love to me. Come and get me, I whispered. In England, come and get me.

We had said our goodbyes in New Amsterdam. I had made some pretext about returning, offered to collect the rent, some *story*. I caught a hire car from the rank outside Stabroek market, travelled back by myself along that long East Coast road wedged in-between a fat Indian woman, numerous bags, two men. I'd sat forward on the frayed leather seat, prepared for the pot-holes. Coconut palms swayed in the triangles of blue between elbow and window. From the *Torani* steamer, the rooftop of your house glinted across the water.

I'd popped to Mrs J's; Mummy had told me to stay with her, not to stay in our house alone, but by the time Mummy found out the truth I would be far away in England. "Mummy's fine with me staying alone", I told her airily, "after all, she's sending me half way round the world by myself!"

You'd come and whistled as you always had, from the gate, and I appeared, making my movements deliberately slow, lounging back on the porch rail like I imagined Judy Geeson would, or Hayley Mills, or Tuesday Weld or any of those stars people were always telling me I looked so much like. But you were top-class lounge lizard material.

You walked more slowly up those stairs than it took cassareep to drip from the bottle, the cigarette glowing between your fingers, sweat darkening the armpit of your chocolate brown shirt.

We didn't even consider Mummy's bed. Her crucifix would have impaled us. We didn't use mine either. Small and narrow, with Aunt Lel just across the road? So we went into my sisters' double bed at the back of the house, the dounze tree silent. That bed that had, once upon a time, widened for my sisters and me and visiting cousins, sleeping up to four crossways. That bed that, before my upgrade to the gallery room, had seen countless pillow fights; that, through thin walls, had heard Mummy giving birth to Yonnette; that, Christmas upon Christmas, would hear us whispering at foreday morning; that had had its share of small tousled heads, curly-haired, hard-haired heads, snoring mouths and dribble mouths, brown arms flung wide, punching and kicking and tossing off sheets, talcum powder smell and poopsy smell, fever burning up times, Limacol times, calling the doctor times. In that bed you told me how much you would miss me and asked how I could leave you. The smell of your damp skin in the late afternoon heat mixed with that aftershave you wore was imprinted on my sister's pillow. I sat astride you feeling a mixture of sadness and power. All those times you had hurt me, when I had sent my little prayers up to Jesus, all that detailing in my diary of the past eighteen months, those depths of despair, that rare bliss when I loved you so much you were every corpuscle in my blood, came back and inhabited the pores of my skin like rain.

Your coarse hands pinned my thighs down as if they never ever wanted to let me go. But even then, as my eyes refused to leave yours, even then as part of my brain was fixing these moments in my memory for eternity, something else inhabited me. That same something that had left pencil smudges on my fingers and thumbs, guided outlines of dancing figures onto white paper, teased a softness onto the pencilled mouth of a young girl – some migrant Pre-Raphaelite beauty. That same something that made me copy out song lyrics, head bent to the radio to catch the words, shouting at my sisters to shut up. The Hollies, Hot Chocolate, Otis Redding, The Moody Blues.

Those snatches of poetry, copied out onto the inner pages of school books – Tennyson: 'O what shall I be at fifty, if I am still alive, if I find the world so bitter when I am but twenty-five...' Well before you, all of Grimm's, The Snow Queen, The Famous Five. The Hardy Boys, Anne of Green Gables, What Katy Did. Little Women...All of that world that lived and breathed inside me that you were no part of.

I didn't know then of our own Caribbean literatures, but buried my nose into the delicious smell of library books, new books, borrowed books, comics; re-enacted those tales for myself and my sisters to perform our own version of Little Women with me as Meg, Des as Jo, Mary as Beth and Yonnette as Amy...

What did you know or care about those narratives embedded into my very fabric? And you see, it mattered, it so, so mattered, because my heroes were given to me on paper, on screen, James Dean smouldering, Warren Beatty and Natalie Wood tormented by passion in 1961 in *Splendour in the Grass*, Scarlett and Rhett, Dr Zhivago.

Mills & Boon novels had prepared me for you, the dark, disagreeable hero with a tongue for a sword, but we both knew, at some level, that no-one had written us a script. Would I be the career girl in New Amsterdam, in Georgetown? Was I secretary material, mother material? Would I stay home and mind kids? And if we wanted to lift the umbrella even higher, could I marry you? Could Catholic marry Muslim?

Who would I vote for? D'Aguiar? Burnham? Jagan? More and more my mother, my sisters and I were feeling we had no place. New Amsterdam was becoming a ghost town. Marix was gone, Elly, Barbara, Joey, Latch, Frencho, Vidya. Our arms were getting tired waving goodbye to all our friends. America, you whispered, America.

Our friend Hazel had organised a farewell party at her house in Georgetown. The house was full of people, my girlfriends from New Amsterdam, Georgetown boys, family, you. Somebody was putting records on, people were dancing. I see Katie push through the crowd to the DJ and whisper in his ear. He nods, then puts on Jefferson Airplane 'I'm leaving on a jet plane'. Everybody claps and Katie pulls you out from the dance you were having with Lorna, drags you over to me. You're protesting, "Leave me nuh!" But the whole room is watching. So you take me in your arms unwillingly and the crowd cheers again, singing along heartily as if it was a birthday party. But you're angry. You didn't want to come. You dance with me with one arm hanging by your side, a cigarette glowing brightly between your fingers.

And so I go. When the plane lifts and I look down and see my country below me for the first time, I wonder where all the houses and all the roads have gone. All I can see is a wave of green bush rolling away and away inland with thin brown squiggles which are rivers; beyond that, the ocean. It's as if everything I've ever known has been swallowed up. I've said everything I had to say to you. I speak to Daddy now – I'm flying, Daddy, I'm flying.

And you, my country, return to me when it rains; this English rain now borrows the force of the Trade Winds and pelts bangalang, down on conservatory, slate roofs, tiles.

There was a time I wished for rain such as this, laughing at English rains and rivers, rivers no more than streams. *You want to see rain?* I would laugh. This could be with the girls in the factory, as we stood outside the workshop doors and watched the water run down the concrete yard. And they would look at each other and laugh, drawing on the last stumps of their cigarettes before the bell sounded. Or pausing on a bridge in the Kent countryside, to play Pooh Sticks on a swirl of water barely above the level of its stones. Try the Demerara, or the Berbice, *those* are rivers!

You return to me when babies come, cut out of me with knives, their eyes bluer than the Guyana sky, and I sing *You will know that you are down in Demerara, Demerara, you will know that you are down in Demerara* and *Clap hands for Mamma*, and *Brownskin girl, stay home and mind baby*...and the rain bangalangs on the conservatory roof and no-one but me will know what it means.

You return to me when I re-enter a classroom at the age of thirty-nine into a room swimming with the faces of strangers and I feel as stupid and fragile and as tongue-tied as I was first time round, the tongue only free within the pages of a diary, and when I am asked what my name is I temporarily forget, then wonder what accent should I use...and there you are again, my country, tripping off the edge of my lips, pushing your rain-smell earth-smell in, hysterically whispering *Latin Latin Creole Creole English Southern Counties*. And mothering and lovering and factory floors and washing floors and divorce courts had never been my intention.

And you return to me each time I have to peel you off my lips, explain where you are geographically, culturally, politically, and always have to explain why I am here and not there, *all that sunshine innit?* and I still don't know the answer. And you return to me when that telephone call comes all the way from Georgetown just before I leave to get the kids from school one wet December afternoon, 1999, *Georgetown calling*...Al Creighton from the University of Guyana telling me I have won the Guyana Prize.

And I wear you always, like that nugget ring I have hidden about myself, and where once I returned in the smallest of shapes, a firefly or a kiskadee, a raindrop even, or the pinhead of a memory, I now return in poems, and in these stories told so long ago; and hope no-one will think I am a jumbie and find a shell to break me with.

# 1

# The Conch Shell

*1969*

We throw it down the backsteps and watch it bounce, clatter and splinter, heading for the yard. All them years on top of the Phillips radio, *Mister King Conch*, always needing dusting. Now he just drop like somebody old shoe, and for the first time we hear Mummy cursing bad words. Daddy spirit was *in* the shell, they said, he didn't know yet he was dead. Mr Dead had come up and catch him unawares, with no chance to get ready nothing. So back to the land of the living he'd come; or even he never left. He bring back the smell of the funeral flowers and perfume, and frighten us into running out the house to sleep with Aunty Jean, or Aunty Millie. So, *throw way something that belang to he*, they said. That something was the conch shell. That prize conch he always say come from Barbados, that he used to hold up and blow, ghostly eerie cry like bad news coming, till he put it to we ears and we listen to the ocean rushing. Now we too cursing after it like hellfire, because is curse you have to curse the ghost so he can know he not welcome here. And although part of we feeling sorry for we Daddy trap up in there, there was a certain *licentiousness,* that pleasure we had to cuss, as previous to that we can't even say *Damn* or *O God* for fear of licks or a mouth wash out with soap.

"You *Rass!*" I bellow, liberated.

But Mummy, eyes red and knuckles white, pull me up sharp.

"That's enough, Margaret!" she scold. "Quite enough."

# 2

# Wheeling

*1966*

Teenage girls weave their bicycles through the narrow streets of New Amsterdam, Berbice, in our El Dorado country, once *Guiana, Land of Many Waters*. We are independent now, with a new name, Guyana.

I am riding my new Raleigh Daddy just bought me, after a year at Berbice High School. It stood on the bridge outside our front gate, black, gleaming, silver spokes and pedals glinting in the sun. My father waited on the front porch for my gratitude. My younger sister Desiree had got hers first but no matter. *Clever puss*. She didn't waste a whole year at a posh school and get sent home in disgrace. My tongue had got stuck to the roof of my mouth, something that often happened when my father was around. I'd stood with my head hanging down, looking at the wheels.

Daddy had got vexed and snapped, "You going to say thanks for the bicycle?" He looked down at me, sucking his teeth, then waved me away to fetch him a glass of milk. But away from his piercing grey eyes, his forbidding presence, his lashing tongue and fast hand with the cane, my own tongue broke loose and there I go, cruising with my girlfriends from school – Lorna, Devi, Elly, Barbara, Katie, the twins, and the American, Glory; them-say-she-say story going nine to the dozen. It may or may not be one moment in time, but over five years, from 1967 to 1971 there was not one week would go by that Margaret Harris and some girlfriend would not be rolling those wheels bumptiously over hot concrete.

This is our hometown. We were all born here, apart from Glory; with ancestors from Europe, Asia and Africa. Prior to being ruled by the British, our little town had been owned by the Dutch, hence all the Dutch place names. To outsiders she was just another town on the banks of a river, galvanised roofs glinting in the sun. A brown-skinned town, a red-skinned town, an ash-black town; born of exploration and exploitation, slavery, coffee, tobacco, cane. But that's not the town we knew. Our town, our world, was one of friends, parents, school and what you were or were not allowed to do.

The Berbice River rushed to meet her wolf-father Mister Atlantic. He had brought her all her children, patrolled our horizons, from his past of sailing ships and slave ships to his present majesty of containers and liners. You spied the gleam of him, the shining ocean-top of him, as he hung there so many miles above us. We watched him from the stelling (the Dutch word for *pier*), the river opening her mouth wide to greet him.

New Amsterdam is still a new town. Before 1790 she was simply Bush. Jungle. Mouth of the river. Brown water a mile wide, heat mist thick on both banks rolling away inland full of don't-know-what-name trees. Home to monkey, parrot, labba; jaguar. Amerindians. Runaway slaves. Before that the capital of Berbice was Nieuw Amsterdam, some seventy miles upriver, claimed and settled in 1627 by one Mynheer Abraham van Pere, a Dutchman.

In 1763 the slave Cuffy organised the Berbice Slave Rebellion, blazing a trail along the banks of the Berbice River, including Fort Nassau. The colonial powers twigged then that the mouth of a river is the place for a town to be.

From 1803 Britain took control.

Our river was a border and a highway between country, town, and Bush. Between up-there people and down-there people. The city-slickers lived in Georgetown seventy miles away, whilst along the river descendants from plantations and Guiana's original inhabitants farmed, fished and wrestled the forest. Sugar-cane and rice fields rolled over the Canje River and the traces of rebellion, tended on the whole by Indian descendants of Indentureship.

That river informed the entire sense of our positioning, geographic and social: we were *country gurls*. For many of us it was just something to be crossed, a pathway to somewhere else.

The stelling itself was a place to take the breeze: it jutted out into the brown waters, the liming place to watch the ferry, eye up its passengers, imagine a crossing.

I loved every opportunity to cross that river, whether it was to take the launch over to Blairmont Estate, head for grown-up Georgetown, or travel up to Kwakwani with my father on the tug.

At thirteen, a night stay in Devi's house across the river was the height of excitement for me. Their Hindu Gods, Ganesh and Lakshmi, figures of fascination for me, resided on an altar garnished with offerings of rose petals and rice; so different from mine, plainly adorned with the doleful St Theresa, the Infant Jesus of Prague and my mascara.

For many people the river was a workhorse: fishermen and loggers, estate workers, sawmill owners. At Everton with the Reynolds Bauxite Company, she ruled my father's life with her tides. She was there at his birth in 1908.

Silent witness and companion to wilderness, a carrier of myth and legend from Sir Walter Raleigh onwards, containing a water-memory of explorers and native peoples who depended on and survived her. Early adventurers sailing in on her tides or hacking through her jungle would not have imagined the perspective of the river, or of those with a ripple of unknown unpronounceable names who gazed narrow-eyed from between the trees. *Akawois, Warrous*...From the sixteenth century onwards, adventurers with a fever in their hearts for the unknown had left women and mapped routes to follow the myth of El Dorado. They would slash, possess and rename in their own and others' glory, falling victim to ticks, venomous snakes, and arrows tipped with curare, in the total absence of anything resembling their previous reality.

But us schoolgirls now, with History drummed into us at school – the standard, European version, complicated by a mass of named overseas battles, dates and treaties, boring shenanigans far removed from our reality – we just dreamed of break time and an ice pole from the tuck-shop. At the fringes of our imaginations lingered stories heard over the parents' rum and cokes, of missionaries who'd braved the Bush to bring the light, armed only with the Bible, mirrors and beads; of Mittleholzer's sword that had helped to vanquish the slave Cuffy's rebels just up the road there between those trees, behind that creek. Apart from the secrets, we also heard what which government party was doing to who, and Education, Education, Education. But of course *she* lived, History did, in each and every face, whose colour, like those on colonial maps, marked us like sheep dye.

This was a going-places time, a forget-all-that-rubbish time, and apart from a brief memory of speedboat racing, and myself high up on Daddy's shoulders watching the boats bounce on the spray from the safety of the stelling, for me and others like me the river was just *there* to be crossed.

Only later would the feeling grow that she was not a plaything, as all who disrespected her found out again and again – somebody would get their leg or life sliced by an outboard engine, would fall overboard off some craft or simply become a sacrifice in the wash and wake of countless others. And much later still would images and imaginings of other ships surface, of salt sea captains thumbing ships' logs listing coffee, tobacco, human cargo.

So cross her as swift as you can, whether it be on the Torani, or the Blairmont launch which frequently bore a volume of passengers double her own indeterminate size. Or with these thoughts in the future to come, or the bridge I hear they have built now. And later, child, later, when you are living in that country introduced to you through history books, realise that the two men through whom your awareness of and propensity for love and loss was experienced, had one other thing in common apart from you: this river; and the fact that your daddy born and grow near that other, first capital of Berbice, way up the river, Fort Nassau. There, within spitting distance of emancipated plantations, your daddy would run and play on sandbanks bounded by the tides. Your lover too would wake and sleep with her smug slow passage in his ear.

But for now we cycle. From my street, St John Street, along Water Street. Our bikes are stallions, flags, beacons: Moultons, Choppers, Raleighs. They told the world you'd passed your exam. That one bringing up the rear with its mudguard clanking spoke volumes.

We rolled, like scores of other teenagers for whom the bicycle was a cruising machine a step up from Shank's pony, past the families strolling round town late afternoon, taking part in the official activity of Window Shopping. Past Barclays Bank, the new Faaz cinema, D.M. Fernandes, New Amsterdam market, the Town Hall, Bata shoe store, J.P. Santos...These are the days still where shops have counters and stern-looking assistants standing behind them and asking what you want. There is no wandering up and down aisles. In Wrefords the lady takes your money and places it in a silver pot that swings madly across the ceiling to the office upstairs. Zing! And change and receipt come swinging back. So you dream harder and longer about the things you think you want, press your nose close to the glass at J.P. Santos where Lordy! a battery-operated Monkee mobile sits, pink as candyfloss, the heads of Davy, Micky, Mike and Peter protruding from fake leather seats. Roll on pass the Penguin Hotel, Bacchus Photography Studio, Bookers Stores. Legs slow to allow gear changes, stretch to stand on the pedals, pause to freewheel. Arms let go of handlebars: *Watch this, man!*

Wearing a creative collage of what was fashionable, what was allowed, and what was affordable, Elly with her shirt dress and chain belt, thick black ponytail, not allowed to wear a miniskirt. Devi not allowed to expose her midriff, tying the ends of her shirt baring her brown belly to the sun. Me, hampered by the thinnest legs New Amsterdam had ever seen, diverting attention from them with halter tops and hippie bead necklaces hanging between cotton-wool cleavage. Glory, being American, the freest of us all, in short shorts...but what could you expect from someone who undressed bold as brass *outside* the dressing-room at Blairmont swimming pool whilst we fumbled under towels and behind closed doors?

Pass the Globe cinema where on a Saturday afternoon East Indians filed in to see movies from their mother country, dressed to the nines in shalwars and saris, home-made dresses, gold bangles and silver sandals; the young men, not to be outdone, in bright shirts, seamed pants, gold teeth and rings.

These are the children of Indenture, past citizens of Madras and Lahore, Calcutta and Delhi. The movies take them back to an ancestral past where the Indian landscape was as much a star as Lata Mangeshkar and Shammi Kapoor: lovers chased each other through paddy fields and rivers, peered at each other through the cracks of temples to a musical soundtrack that reverberated through the walls of the cinema and echoed along the wooden stelling and the bank of the river. When the doors opened the audience stumbled out into the sunlight on Water Street, shocked by the light and the strangeness of this reality.

We talk of school and boys, of parents who were bad-minded and unfair, of periods. We sang out in Guyanese patois, discouraged by parents and teachers who constantly reiterated the need for speaking proper English, which no, does *not* include Americanised slang.

We laugh at the old man "with he goady hanging ova he bicycle seat", at the English duck who just come back from abroad with quack quack in her voice, at limeys who eat curry and roti with a knife and fork.

Pass the drinks factory, juddering over the wooden slats of the stelling underneath where crabs dance the bossa-nova in the green mud at twilight and bathe their silvery hildren when the tide comes in. Brown river water and Coca-Cola tops, diesel oil, cigarette packets, eels, worms and shrimps whirling and waltzing as the river froths against the greenheart posts. We girls lean on our bikes, wishing we had the extravagance of sunshades; the sunlight cuts the water sharp as cutlasses.

The ferry docks, the circular steel floor on the car deck spins, vehicles nose out onto the ramps, car horns blow.

Foot passengers, too impatient to wait for the doors on the passenger deck to open and align with the pontoon, clatter down the inside steps, push their way through the queuing traffic. Motorbikes with lean, hungry boys sporting sunshades scream Yamaha and Suzuki souls out into the afternoon, weaving snakelike and fearless towards Water Street.

Escaped logs from Fazal's sawmill spin past in the wake of the Torani. Mistress Berbice bears them like bounty, gifts of appeasement, as she carries camoodies and crabs, bauxite, and bones.

She carries stories too, so many that a lifetime of reading wouldn't be enough. But maybe reading's not the thing, though they beat *that* into children's heads up and down the country. Most stories live on the edges of lips, or in the indentation of a rosary bead on the palm; through the cracks of a bedroom door, the shape of a footprint; or are simply biological: cells and chromosomes, grey eyes in a coconut face, a natty dread trembling from a forehead, a mouth pursed to suck a star-apple. And though I didn't know it, the trembling of them was present in my very knees and thumbs, belly and anklebones.

Devi is telling a story...of a water nymph near her village who cries from the bottom of an old well where she got trapped when the Dutch left, and from which no-one will draw water now. She draws gasps from us. "You lie!" We rail at her. "Is stupidness!" But she just shrugs, straightens her shirt and heads for the ferry. "Ah gone."

From Water Street to the Botanical Gardens, a green oasis from the blaze of the sun, a respite from the clatter of vehicles and blasts of car horns. Circle the path round Queen Victoria's statue, veer off onto paths littered with hibiscus and oleander petals, the brown edges of coconut fibres. Under the palms a doe-eyed girl disappears with a boy towards the bandstand, her left hand swinging by her side. *Going to steal a kiss under the monkey puzzle tree?* Purple bougainvillea confetti the lawn where, eyes out for the attendant, we wheel our bicycles across to the manatee pond. Blue dragonflies hover above Victoria Regia lilies; lilies as large as rafts, and unique to our Amazonian continent. I dream of being small enough to settle into one and drift away across this deep dark pond. A woman and a small boy crouch there, soo-sooing, coo-cooing. We join the chorus, hands ready with vegetation to feed the resident manatee, and at last she appears, regal as a queen, nose rising between the lilies, then her whole head, eyes resting, slow and wise, on her callers.

From the Gardens we cruise Queen Elizabeth Avenue, riding past our school, wondering whether to continue up past the madhouse and lime up Canje Bridge. Glory lifted her bottom up past the school auditorium.

"Bum to you!" she laughed. We crack up. We'd never known anyone with such disdain for everything we'd been taught was sacred. Past the big posh houses with the long drives. The white house with the mango tree where that woman with the sad face lived behind the shutters of the jalousie.

It was Glory who had noticed her one school morning, her elbows on the windowsill, her eyes fast on children going to school.

"What she looking at, eh?" Glory had quipped, in her new acclimatised Guyanese patois. She had openly bared her blue eyes up at the woman, looking back even as she cycled past. Her audacity impressed and scared me at the same time.

Morning after morning it evolved into a pattern: us staring at the woman we noticed was always there, looking out of the window. Then one day she noticed. She became aware of us casting our eyes up as we cruised past...No, lemme rephrase that: the woman knew it was barefaced staring she was dealing with, and that really got her goat. Children do not stare adults in the face! The abuse that flew out of the window frightened the pigeons out of the tree and nearly caused us to fall off our bikes. "What y'all staring at, you blasted vipers? You want me come see you headmaster?!"

She leaned out of the window as she hollered and I noticed how pasty her arms looked, as if she'd just come back from abroad, or else somebody shut her up all the time in the house. "Nothing here for you!" she carried on, "you hear me?!" She pulled her head in like a frightened tortoise, slamming the jalousie shut.

"Eh-eh!" we exclaimed. We were stunned, and carried on up the road on wobbly bicycles, chattering ten to the dozen. *Who she rass think she is?* But we kept our glances sidelong from then on. She was obviously a mad woman, or some Dutch white ghost. In any case none of us wanted her marching into Mr Beharry office. Eh-eh. She rass. Like they said, *there were more mad people out than in.*

We cruise on down Main Street, stop for a howdy-do at the new Nazarene church standing back from its elegant stretch of lawn which was *the* cool place to be: new pastor, handsome white son Jimmy B who I tease at school with an endless rendition of Dusty Springfield's 'Son of a Preacher Man'.

When he got me vex one time on a school trip to see sugar-cane make into molasses I throw stinging nettle on him, see his nice white skin turn red.

Carry on past the Methodist church, the Anglican church...for a small town New Amsterdam had more than its share of churches: Catholic, Mission Chapel, Seventh Day Adventist, Baptist, Lutheran...*imagine, all those years ago they had floated the old one down the river on rafts from Fort Nassau!* And that wasn't counting Jehovah's Witnesses, Temples, Mosques and all those without name carrying on in night-time backyards with clap hands, drums and white fowl, obeah-dobeah. The place more holey than strainer. Chu's Ice Cream Parlour was bookstore, cake-shop and general liming establishment: *the* place to slide onto a bar stool and eat ice-cream whilst you eyed the talent liming by. This is where you hear who was sooring who, who was holding a fête, who somebody see up Backdam when they told their mother they were going market. Here those nice VSOs smoothed their polished bottoms and roughed up their accents and became fourteen and sixteen and laughed loudly and improperly as they sucked milkshakes up fat straws. The pavement with its offering of motorbikes: slow your pedals...*uh huh awhoo dat in dere gurl!*

Pass the Gaiety Cinema with its posters advertising its usual mediocre films: Lee van Cleef snarling, holster at the ready, Jane Russell's bosoms spilling out. I nevah forget that time I see true to God a man turn into a gorilla there. As He is my witness. School took us there, a long line of us from primary school, heads burning in the hot sun, filed into Gaiety Cinema one afternoon. We went straight downstairs into Pit, which was ordinarily for poor people who hollered and stamped the ground as soon as cowboys or Elvis start buffing each other. Was theatre for true. Ordinarily was House we headed for, not Balcony, unless somebody else was paying for you. But there we were all sitting quiet in the dark when a cage was rolled in with a man who, and I do not lie, changed before our eyes into a gorilla. Scream? You nevah hear commotion so! Girls held onto girls, hid their faces in each others' shoulders, covered their eyes with their hair. The boys, after a preliminary jumping out of their skin, whooped like marauding Apaches. The cinema proprietor then calmly asked us if we would like to see the transformation reversed. "YES!" yelled the terrified girls. "NO MAN, LEAVE HE SO!" hollered the boys. And right before our eyes the gorilla shrunk back into the skin of a man.

Fried chicken and noodles get us drooling past the Chinese restaurant, as do the boys loitering at the top of Pitt Street, where rock steady music was rolling out of an upstairs window and *those kind of women* leaned out. Two of the boys are wearing white T-shirts with tight short sleeves like Marlon Brando. They lean up against shop doorways smoking cigarettes from long arms.

Cruise past streets named after other places, kings, queens and the church: Pope and Kent, Trinity, Coburg...others with a hint of forgotten history like Lad Lane...The three main roads running parallel to the river were criss-crossed by dozens of narrow streets, along which gutters laid out by the Dutch ran under individual bridges leading to our yards.

We pause at Gajraj Sawh's General Store, pull into the forecourt where TJ leans against someone's Yamaha and says *Y'all girls liming eh? You going to the fête Satday nite? You mummy and daddy goon loow you to go?* He looks straight at Elly, but she only has eyes for Mao thundering past on his red motorbike. Some busybody rushes by wearing church hat and clutching a bible: *Y'all girls ain't got homes to go to?*

Soon the news will fly, this *News* Amsterdam with every mouth a carrier pigeon, how the Captain daughter loitering outside Gajraj Sawh talking to Boy. The carrier pigeon won't know of the time I picked up a small-small kitten from this same forecourt. It was wandering through the bales of cloth and nobody know whose it was, some stray, and I took it home, close to my chest as I steered my bike with one hand; took it home and spoon-fed it milk from my baby sister's Cow & Gate spoon and tucked it up warm in a box under my bed on top of Daddy's guitar case with all the loose sheets of music and next morning when I reached down half-asleep and smiling, my hand touched cold stiff fur and I recoiled screaming. But then that had nothing to do with anything.

Down Pope Street, under the shadow of the Catholic Church. Elly's brothers and sisters swing on the gatepost like monkeys, her mother's watchful eyes staring down from an upstairs window. *Gotta go make tea* Elly says reluctantly and laughs as usual, her brown eyes holding a world defined by Indian-ness, schooling, hard work and new Christianity. The rest of us veer across the pot-holes to the Backdam.

This is the road where New Amsterdam's self-assurance as a town reminds itself that Bush not long gone. He waiting at the edges remembering his glory days before the cutlasses come. Never mind the new post office; He waiting there behind the trench, behind the houses, behind the stretch of pasture where branded cows wander and dark treetops brush the skyline. Vines wrap round the jamoon trees, and ants' nest rampaging underground waiting their own turn to take back the world. Jiggers wait, blowflies wait, ringworm waits. But now the boys dive in the trench like seals, and from front verandas Portuguese, black, dougla and Indian women sit in their rockers or sweep up the leaves from concrete and mud-yards where tamarind seeds fall. There's a smell of cow dung from the field and the telegraph wires have trapped the memory of Easter Sunday's kites: all that singing in the sky now are shreds of tissue paper and kite-strings fluttering from the tops of trees.

There are two schools yonder, beyond Bush's sapodilla head and the heads of immigrant palms and breadfruit trees...Vryman's Erven and the Berbice Educational Institute (BEI), where tarmac is starting to show that Bush, after all, will be king. I very nearly went to BEI. My mother and I walked up that long-long road where wood and concrete swum in the distance against an impressionist background. I don't know what happened then, except that I ended up going, happily, to Berbice High, which had the edge, like it or not. Everybody thought their school was the best, of course, and always some schoolgirl somewhere would be leaning on a bridge or a street corner ready to hiss about those who think their shit don't stink or who mother must be sleep with a crapaud to give birth to somebody so ugly let-me-name-no-names.

Glory is drawling on about the new boy come up from Georgetown, having him over to listen to records, and our eyes open wide: *On you own? By yourself?!* and I tried to imagine Daddy's face if boys came up our front steps, how he would raze my backside with the wild cane. Remembering him now, and seeing that all of a sudden the afternoon was cooling down, we spin our bicycles round like steeds and head back into Main Street, the twins turning into their driveway by the hospital, Lorna into Kent Street, me into St John Street.

# 3

# All Colours Under the Sun

*Say 'coloured,' dear.*
*Black, white, pink and red. Yellow plantain, green.*
*Chinee, coolie, dougla, buck. Shiny tamarind seed.*
*Whitey shitey, penny a glass*
*If you don't want it, kiss me ass.*

Elizabeth, my mother, is Portuguese and 'white'. The distinction is not ours. Her grandfather, Sidney Hawker, a Scotsman, arrived in British Guiana sometime in the late 1800s. Travelling with him was his son, my grandfather Cyril. There's no wife and mother named. There are no records, no family Bible with lineage carefully inscribed with each birth and death. A fire in Georgetown in the early 1900s destroyed many official records, and then there's the woodants. But they there: true-true, blue eyes, photographs and a yard full of children. They had white men's jobs...Sidney, a plantation manager at Alness Estate in Berbice, Cyril, later, an overseer at Diamond Estate, then chief engineer for the Sea Defence on that Georgetown seawall I would lime on with motorbike boys in my own time, taken for granted now by so many lovers and gangsters. The seawall Cyril worked on faint-heartedly holds back the Atlantic Ocean prowling like a leopard six thousand feet above.
We don't know what memories my great grandfather and his son might have had of Scottish Highlands or Glasgow tenements, whether their background was smog, mills, or mining; if their passage to British Guiana was due to adventuring, economic betterment, religious intolerance or a result of the clearances. The Scotland we knew came to us in school, through the poetry of Robert Burns. It came to us in films which imprinted the words *kilt*, *Highlands* and *haggis*. Would they have carried the Scottish brogue on their

tongues, in their ears or minds? Would they have missed the clean chill of a Scottish winter or a grudging springtime on moorland heather? How did they feel about being white in British Guiana in those still-unequal times? Thousands of Scots came to British Guiana. The coast was littered with plantations like Alness and Rosehall, named after Scottish villages and estates of the plantocracy. How did they feel about Africans; about the slave trade whose legacy they became part of? It is possible to imagine ships and salty tongues, and an ocean rolling. It is possible to imagine fear at a great expanse of water, with no sight of land past the Azores. They may have worked the land, or come from poverty. So many deserted the United Kingdom. That my great grandfather and his son travelled together does not indicate criminal stock to me; rather that of the adventurer, or the hopeful migrant seeking his fortune on new, warmer shores. If one is free to plunge into the hazardous unknown with a small child, surely only excitement or need could be the lure?

Nothing is known of my great-grandmother, which may well suggest that any of these reasons could have propelled the decision to emigrate. As a long shot Sidney could have simply taken the boy and left Scotland! But I can't see that. What single man would choose to travel halfway round a nineteenth century world with a child? They might even have begun the trip as a family, and my mysterious great-grandmother simply did not make it. The Atlantic holds so many millions close to her womb...She's lost to history, like so many in the tales told of these new lands that Raleigh and all those adventurers had died for.

My grandfather Cyril grew up in British Guiana from about the age of seven. Did you run wild, Scottish Grandpa? Were you friends with white boys, black boys, Indian boys? Did you play cricket on unmade roads with a homemade bat and a rubber ball? Were you a loner, the little Creole boy red-kneed on a porch on the edge of a canefield, a black cook bringing you lime juice and handing your weary father a rum? There are stories of half-brothers and sisters, not quite as white as you...The black cook **was** real and those children **were** real: Jack, Annie, Adelaide, Charlie...How was that

Guiana of the nineteenth century, that you lived in? You wouldn't have needed to flee that red land that had tied your black brothers who walked off as soon as. Slavery had been abolished some fifty years. Did your accent change? Did the way of life ever become natural? Me and my friends now, how natural it is to swing from Creole to propa English; our souls can split to house so many selves, and tongues.

My grandfather: was he Catholic or Protestant? I've only just learned about Protestant Madeirans, and Scots who had moved to Madeira in pursuit of freedom to worship: two groups who became yet another band of immigrants to the West Indies. Cyril would eventually marry a Madeiran woman, my mother's mother, Evelyn.

As privileged as Cyril's position might have been, by merely having white skin in British Guiana, if he was Catholic, that would have been as bad, in English eyes, as being Portuguese! The snobbery of the English ruling class looked down on this merchant class, who had come in their droves in the mid-eighties. So, Cyril, a young man thinking this his country, knowing little of Scotland or of his reception there should he ever return...did he cast his eye around Demerara for a marriage partner whose social standing would complement his own? What were your choices, Cyril?

This we know: our young man with the keen blue eyes spotted Beauty lingering at the water pump in Golden Grove village.

A Portuguese young woman by the name of Angela Carmelita Petronella Brazh, birth date Valentine's Day, 1898. Yes, *Angela*, daughter of Rosa. Angela's father had died and Rosa had married again to a Mr Machado, producing another daughter, Evelyn, in 1906. *Aha* ...

Cyril is entranced by Angela's thick lustrous hair, her dancing brown eyes. *Marry me*, he whispers, leaning down off his mare one morning on his way to the sugar factory. Slavery had been abolished, but overseers were still in work; indentured servants from India now laboured on the estates.

Angela didn't have eyes for the ivory-skinned horseman. Feisty, strong-willed, and passionate, she must have suspected his brooding nature did not match hers. Or looked to a future instead of the past. She had her sights set further along the canefield, down that track where a fierce young black man worked on the land. He had taken to coming into the shop she ran with her mother Rosa. There was something about him...

Angela didn't like the way the overseer was blocking the sun on the space she stood. Even when his horse shifted, she didn't like the way she had to shield her eyes from the sun to see him, or that she had to raise her eyes to him. So, thanks but no thanks; and in the following weeks that other caller came melting out of the night, causing consternation in the holier-than-thou Portuguese Catholic household. For not only was this Brian James a black man, he already had a woman, and children, mimicking the pattern that four centuries of slavery had imprinted on Africans.

Who knows what ancestral memories burned behind *his* eyes? Did he remember families, thatched villages, ships and chains? Did he remember the slave port Goree, other tongues and gods...Shango, Yemanja...herds of wildebeest, elephants, the songs of goatskin drums? No-one apart from our teachers and political parties spoke of slavery. My father does not take me aside and say, "Margaret girl, let me tell you a bit about our history and how the black man has come to walk these streets." No. What you got was the mantra to strive onwards and upwards, the words 'betterment' and 'education' used more frequently than 'history'. Not one member of my extended brown-skinned family would have seen themselves as black.

Now I know that for Africans the notion of family had been usurped by plantation life: tribe torn from tribe, language from culture, children from mothers, sons from fathers, brothers from sisters; all dispersed from plantation to plantation. The white massas took women at will, propagating a flowering of nutmeg and cinnamon coloured children, like me and my sisters, toffee-coloured and chocolate children, children with red hair, green eyes, and irises as dark as those koker dams the Dutch slave masters used to irrigate the fields. Perhaps my father did not know how to say these things; after all, if one is aspiring upwards, one has to leave the past behind.

Brian James was as drawn to Angela as a key to a lock, a

pick to a guitar, a chorus to a hymn. And they would suffer the consequences: estranged from their families, they would move from the County of Demerara to Berbice, then eventually miles upriver to Kwakwani. Off Angela waltzed with Brian, two new Guyanese spirits fused by the old world into an explosive cocktail of colour, class, and religion.

*Of course what better is to be expected of the Portuguese? Aren't they half-Negroid already? Didn't their country throb with Arab and African blood, weren't their caravels and the holds of their ships forever associated with spices and travel to the furtherest corners of the uncivilised world? And their masses, still in the Latin tongue and shaking of incense, how far removed were they from darkest Africa with her mad gods and savage drumming?*

For Brian it was the catalyst he needed to leave the shackles of the land, drop that blasted cutlass and join the new working class, become a policeman in Baggots Town, Demerara, that county whose name would always mean sugar.

Cyril, the rejected suitor, did not stay downcast for long. His eye fell on Evelyn, Angela's younger sister. Who is to know how different his feelings were, how easy it was to shift from one to the other? In such times, how largely would romantic love, as we know it, have featured in these decisions?

Romantic love would be my raison d'être! In my diary I commandeer Tennyson's words from *Maud* as a mantra... 'O what shall I be at fifty, if I were still alive, if I find the world so bitter when I am but twenty-five?' Romantic love would consume me, like the fire consumes the canefields, and all sense would fly, like cane trash, like mad marabunta smoked out of its nest.

Cyril's marriage may have been on the rebound. He may well have weighed up his opportunities with suitable marriage partners. He may well have felt instant passion for Evelyn, been thrilled to marry her, with her fine delicate features and silk-like brown hair. He may even have married her to stay close to Angela. Who knows? As things turned out, Angela indeed was the key, in ways that no-one would have imagined.

Cyril, like Brian, had had other partners, and already had

several other children: Ivan, Irma, Northcote, Marjorie, Sybil, Ismay, Lucille and Compton. Like Brian, he inherited a pattern of behaviour from Guianese ruling class society. Or else that sun made men, and women, mad with a languorous passion, sending them sprawling wide-legged and flushed as hibiscus over paling fences.

Marry Evelyn he did, this sister said yes, and in the early thirties they settled on the East Coast of Demerara, in Buxton, a village re-creating itself out of former estate land that communities came together to buy.

Villages like Buxton, Plaisance and Golden Grove contained a mix of new Guianese as well as Africans, racial terms like 'dougla', 'coloured', 'mulatto' and 'Potagee' becoming part of our language.

Buxton is where Cyril's son Albert was born to him and Evelyn in 1933, followed by Eloise Dolores Elizabeth, my mother, in April 1935.

I only know Buxton from passing through it on the train. We would have disembarked from the Torani at Rosignol, and she would have been waiting, pawing the ground like a buffalo, steam crowning the tops of the blue trees before she made her chuff-chuff way over the greenheart sleepers. The journey would have steamed us through the banana plantations, where the fat wide leaves brushed her as she passed, and we were warned not to stick our arms out *in case cutlass man chop you gold bangle*. We would have begged to stand outside and ride like cowboys where the carriages were coupled together, looking over the wild landscape for the cutlass men. We would have crossed the Mahaica Bridge, heads hanging out the window at the waters below; would have been caught up in the excitement of the rush of pedlars onto the train shouting *"fish and bread, fish and bread"* baskets on their heads full of bananas, star-apples, genip and sugar-cake. We would have pointed to the mud houses that squatted on legs in the fields.

When houses began to pocket the landscape and dogs ran alongside the railway line, cyclists slowed at signal crossings, and we passed the Kent Shirt factory, you knew you were nearing the city...

I can imagine Evelyn sitting on one of those front porches,

rocking her new baby girl, that brown-haired, brown-eyes baby.

Her two-year-old son, blond hair shining, spins marbles in the yard.

Every generation looks back and says, "Those were the days!" Here too: "Everybody rub along nice-nice, black, coolie, Chinee, everybody mannerly, stop by, got a good-afternoon for you. There was Respect and everybody free to worship in them own church."

But there is bad-eye too, and bad-mouth. There is need for drumming and rosary and poojah and jaray. There are light-skinned women who always have food on their table, be it just fry bora, shrimps or callaloo, metagee, foo-foo or saltfish.

This woman rocking babies on her front porch never had to rip her hands shredding cane or rubbing some white woman washing, some nasty stain-up sheet over a washboard in enamel basin under the slow froth of coal-tar soap. This woman does not have to rise at dawn to make roti for a man who have to leave before cock-crow and walk to the canefield or rice field, eye still heavy with sleep and arms aching to the bone. In somebody memory will be the picture of similar white-skinned women sitting or standing on verandas. And how easy it is to say "White women ain't got nothing to worry about".

I try to imagine my grandmother Evelyn's own thoughts, second-best at the marriage post, and the fourth in line to bear her husband's children. *I was just waiting for you,* my grandfather might have reassured her; *I was looking for the right woman!* Is she filled with the bliss of her babies, and the love and full attention of her husband? Does she fit in easy with her neighbours, her church folk, wives who may or may not be the same colour or standing?

Or is her heart as hollow as a marrow-bone when a dog is done with it, missing a life whose alternatives she can't quite imagine, but is hinted at in the fine linen in her press passed down from her mother Rosa who had said came from a place called Madeira?

Evelyn knows nothing about Madeira, only that she is inhabiting a space as transient as the breeze, as slimy as okra. Potagee women. Hold you head high, eyes bright. Portugal have a history longer than a turtle's memory, girl. Wasn't it them who first come sailing up the Demerara? Wasn't it them holding on tight to the whole of Brazil, which, when she first saw it on a map her daddy had shown her, looked so big British Guiana looked like a shrimp next to a whale? And all that fancy music coming over the radio! That music from Brazil with men playing guitars with a rhythm she could feel in her foot bottom, mix up with drumming that she could feel in her hip bone! So how come Mrs So-and-So turn her nose up when she see her at church, preferring to invite only the new blood come out from England to her whist drive? Didn't the Pope have more glory than the Crown? Her sister Angela's disgrace had carry far, and deep inside her soul Evelyn was ashamed that she too had turned her head away from her sister when she came to see her.

Evelyn was alone and lonely, and the gap between herself and Doreen over there, plaiting her daughter's hair in corn rows, was as wide as the Essequibo river. And the nature of her thoughts might have begun to eat away and away at her, like something bad she ate, fermenting in her stomach with such force that even Cyril, with the clumsy kindness of colonial men unsure of their place, could not massage away from her temple, nor calm with a glass of liquor.

When Evelyn lay on their bed with a fever, Doreen sent one of her sons to the seawall where Cyril worked, and dispatched her daughter to the doctor in town. Evelyn had become delirious, wandering out onto the veranda in her nightie, getting a worse chill, for the deceiving heat of the tropics is no friend of ague, but takes glory in sucking blood and bone. The doctor, when he came, did so gracelessly, angered at being called out at what should have been the end of his day. In his confusion and wrath, he needled into Evelyn's arms a concoction meant to restart a heart and quickened one that was already racing ahead of its time. She died in Cyril's arms, her brown eyes fading into the blue, her fingers slowly loosening their grip on the lace-edged sheet that Rosa had bequeathed her. Eloise Elizabeth was five months old.

My mother tells us this story over and over again. She sits in the rocking chair by the radio. We never tire of it; we are entranced. We look at the photo of the grandmother we never knew, the mother she never knew. And dark nights lit by lamplight and white women on night-time porches in long nightgowns fill our hearts with fear. We have learned to fear the night, the riders, the howling dogs, the crapauds, the thief men in soft shoes, ole higues burning in bushes. *Jumbie tek her.* That's what I hear. *Bad eye catch her.*

Angela and Brian hotfooted it to Buxton. "Take the boy," a distraught Cyril said, pacing the veranda with cigarette after cigarette. Across the yard Doreen soothed the crying Eloise. Her last baby was not long weaned so she still had milk, and it was no new thing for black women to nurture white-skinned babies.

Angela left her heart in pieces there, her young sister buried in a Buxton graveyard, her baby girl motherless, and Cyril awake into the nights with glass after glass of liquor. She and Brian departed with a ready-made son, to join others of his they had given a home to...Henry, Wallace and James, and the ironies were not lost on any of them: God had not seen fit to bless them with their own child, and Cyril's eye had set first on Angela, and she had refused him, but look now, here she was seven years later, about to raise his son.

Another whiteskin boy travelled across the country, from Buxton to Baggots Town. Another boy for whom first memories would be furred with rhythm and movement, cart wheels clattering, a woman with a soft bosom who looked like his mother but was not her, and a stern-faced black man staring hard into the distance, and of whom he would remain afraid.

Angela watched the small boy circle her back yard. He sought trees under which to hide, not climb as boys should, and he shrunk low to the ground when Brian's voice boomed across the yard. From the brick kitchen Angela's heart reached out to him. It wasn't only his mother he missed, it was his father too, and his baby sister, the smell of Buxton earth, and his favourite marble.

Angela dreamed. Her dreams had defined her life ever since she could remember. Water, water, everywhere. She would wake up screaming, sending Rosa running into the back room she shared with Evelyn. "Ignore her," her second husband said, "is jealous she jealous." But her dreams got sharper, and prophetic. Many times she had no idea of their meaning, but as she grew she learned they would connect in some way with her daytime life and conscious world.

*A chariot carrying her off into the sky.*
Wheel ruts in the yard, a visitor with a message.
*Waking up with a tune on her lips she'd never heard before.*
Gonsalves' boy next door on his mouth organ, the same tune.
*Her First Communion, but she never gets to wear the beautiful white lace dress.*
Riots around Portuguese shops in Georgetown the day she should have had her First Communion.
*Her sister swimming through the muddy waters of the koker.*
Cyril's message that her sister had died.

Her sister Evelyn is cold and six feet under, but she comes to Angela nevertheless. Her tone is condemning.
*Why you only take the boy? Why you left my girl child? Why you only take the boy? Come and get my girl child!*

The dreams leave Angela perspiring, even in the nights when the rain bucketed down on the galvanised roof bringing a chill that raised the hairs off her arm. She turned to the rosary, repeating the entire litany. The words, instead of empowering her, left her as turned-about as before, bringing her daytime visions of an earth trembling with the powerlessness of women. Behind her fear she knew a small guilt had implanted itself into her womb, and was growing daily as a foetus would: from the moment Cyril had looked down at her from the perch on his horse, the sunlight streaming over his shoulders, she knew she had been chosen. Running off with Brian, to the beat of their own footsteps, had been a diversion that had not allowed her to escape her destiny. If anything, it had cemented it: Brian, for all his rough manner and grouchy tone, was the Helpmeet chosen. Clear as day, in the light of her kitchen, she heard her sister's voice again: *Go, and fetch my girl-child.* So went she went. By train or donkey cart, who knows? Walked the hot road into Buxton, headed for Doreen's house. The sound of a crying child reached her before she got there. She opened the gate. There under the house small arms twisted angrily out of a hammock, the cry piercing, the tiny face screaming with rage. She reached down into the hammock and picked my mother up; her diaper was soiled. She went upstairs with the baby in her arms, stopped in the doorway and listened to Doreen scream as she saw her.

"Mrs Hawker! Oh sweet Jesus!"

Angela stood still. "Is me, Doreen, Mrs James."

Doreen crossed herself. "Good Lord Mrs James, I thought was you sister! Y'all same-same!"

"You got a clean diaper? Let me have a clean diaper and then I taking the baby."

"You can't take the baby, Mrs James! Mr Hawker lef her in my care!"

"I taking the baby, Doreen, you tell Mr Hawker that."

Doreen gave her nothing, not a stitch of clothes, not a diaper.

Angela walked to the shop, bought a towel, wrapped my mother in it and walked out of Buxton.

But Evelyn was still not at peace.

Although spirits are not supposed to cross water, this one did.

Through wide-awake eyes Angela would watch her enter the midnight bedroom and cross to the cot where Eloise lay.

Evelyn shifted the mosquito net, lifted the baby to her breast.

"Go now, Evelyn," Angela whispered, "I gon mind you baby, she safe now. Go to your rest my sister."

After many nights, she did.

Two years later Cyril lay on his bed in a fever. The poultice had not drawn the sickness from his body as it was supposed to. The person who had applied it had done so with malice, and burnt him instead.

"Daddy died," his daughter Lucille wrote. "The poorhouse buried him."

Guiana is alive with carrion crows. They sit on the telegraph poles waiting. Their human counterparts take away presses, and Madeiran linen, mahogany sewing machines, and radios. They take away wedding suits, watch as the blue-eyed man gets lowered into Betervawagting Cemetery, as the poor legacy of a small side-table makes its way to Berbice.

Angela and Brian had left Baggots Town and moved to the Corentyne. Now that they had the children, they decided that Georgetown was not a place to bring them up. The city's problems had affected Brian's job as a policeman. He had grown tired of breaking up disputes, particularly when his own people were involved. Each day down at the docks the men waited for work. New immigrants were coming all the while...from India, China, Europe, even the Caribbean islands. Tales of El Dorado still circulated. Gold and diamond seekers came. Prostitutes prowled in Tiger Bay. Adventurers and romantics came, missionaries with fire in their hearts, men seeking new lives. There was talk of war in Europe. Some came running from that news, especially those who had lived through the last one. Conversely, there were those in the then British Guiana, patriotic to the mother country, already making plans to serve her. King Sugar's crown was slipping, as it had been since the end of forced labour; anyone with a bit of money could buy a failing plantation and try to make it work. Many tried. Cries for fairer wages and workers' rights grew louder. Rivalry between the two main racial groups, angered by history, grew more tense. Their representatives, eager for power, and combined in their displeasure at their colonial rulers, had much to argue, fight, march, protest and loot about.

So Brian and Angela gathered the children up and took the train from Demerara to Berbice, seventy miles from the city. Past Kitty, Plaisance, Buxton. Past koker dams and coconut and banana plantations, rice fields, sugar-cane fields, isolated mud huts. Mahaica, Mahaicony Bridge, where the boy leaned out of the train window and watched the swirling waters beneath wondering what it would be like to fall. He wondered where they were going. He wondered what had happened to his father. He knew his mother had died; he had seen her lying there, and watched them put her in the ground, telling him she had gone to Heaven. He hadn't understood that. Heaven was Up; they had put her Down. "You'll understand when you're older," they had told him, pointing at a dove in the tree and saying something about the spirit. He looked at his baby sister sleeping in Mother's arms. She had her face pressed into her bosom. Her hair was dark and straight, not like his. His blond curls touched his shoulder. Daddy J wanted Mother (that's what all the children would call Angela) to cut it. "No," she said, "it's the boy's luck." He didn't like Daddy J. He shouted. His daddy never used to shout. He looked at his sister again. *Will she ever be big enough to play with?*

# 4

# Me

Apart from the huge painting of the Sacred Heart with the eyes that followed you everywhere, and the one of Jesus Knocking On The Door, the sepia photographs of Evelyn and Cyril took pride of place in our front room.

Evelyn poses by a tall table near a potted palm. She's wearing a long cream dress, the type they wore in the twenties and early thirties. You can see it's a studio photo; the Photographic Studios in NA were just like that, with backdrops of misty columns and trailing plants. We went for a sitting once, and my baby sister Mary cried and cried, afraid of the man with the big machine and the flash. You could still see her cry face in that picture, even with Desiree patting her hand. But of course my grandparents' photographs would have been taken in Georgetown.

Evelyn looks just like Mummy, same brown eyes and brown hair, thin lips and straight nose. Not like *mine*, this ugly flat nose that Mummy tried to pull straight every morning. Or my fat pouty lips. I wonder if Evelyn knew she was going to die. How awful if she did. Dreamt it or something. Mother does. Knows things before they happen.

We'd heard the story over and over, never got tired of it. Evelyn dying, Mother and Daddy James fetching Uncle, Evelyn *dreaming* Mother. Funny that, the way Mummy always says *Evelyn* dreamt Mother and not the other way round. But that's Guyanese talk for you.

The more English we learnt at school the more confused we got between Guyanese and English and writing and speaking. "Speak properly. The Queen's English."

My grandfather Cyril stared down at us with his blue eyes and thin moustache. You could see Uncle Albert in him. Sometimes we would wonder if we had any relatives in Scotland. We learnt about Scotland at school, Robert Burns and Hogmanay and haggis, which is supposed to be like black pudding. I quite liked black pudding sometimes if I didn't think about all that blood mixed with rice. We'd done Lochinvar and Bonnie Prince Charlie and Mary Queen of Scots whose *own cousin* Elizabeth murdered her. God. And poor Raleigh, ending up in the doghouse after all his trouble traipsing round the jungle looking for El Dorado for Queen Elizabeth! Is that why she was such a great Queen? Maybe it was because she lost her own mother Anne before she got to know her. Anne Boleyn had her head chopped off. She was so pretty too in the film, that Geneviève Bujold.

Uncle had named his children after his parents. My cousin Cyril was the same age as me, Evelyn two years younger. Evelyn was the spitting image of Mummy, whilst I, her own child, looked nothing like her; how weird is that? "You're the image of your father," Mummy would say, in a tone that struck me as having rather a disappointed edge.

I thought the story of Mummy's early life was beautiful and tragic. That poor-poor baby just five months old and motherless. I would often picture the death-bed scenes of my grandparents. The story seemed to keep changing, hinting of dark forces and intrigue. I'm sure one version had Evelyn being frightened to death on her backsteps by a jumbie. One had her trying to escape Buxton because she thought nobody liked her. One visualised her beautiful brown-haired head rising out of midnight waters to invade Angela's bedroom, raging at her for leaving her girl-baby; her face would be ghostly and glow outside the window. When it came to the reconstruction of Cyril's death-bed scene, the pale and beautiful Evelyn would hover just like one of those angels in my Sunday missal. *You've got too much imagination.*

The first dead thing I had ever seen was the donkey, Charles, at Williamsburg, Corentyne, where Mummy had grown up. It was I, aged seven or eight at the time, who had found him lying as still as a stone in the field at the back. He was lying under the mango tree where he used to shade himself from the sun, and his belly was already swelled up and covered with flies. The cart he used to pull leaned up by the fence.

The second dead body I saw was a baby, but I don't want to dwell on that now.

The Corentyne.

I can close my eyes and it rushes back to me like that breeze, sharp through the open car window. That long-long country road, the pot-holes, the dust and mud, flat fields, skinny cows, coconut trees, prayer flags. Trips to see Mother and Daddy J, Mummy's old schoolfriends and Uncle Beau and Aunt Carmelita...

Before my Daddy got his pick-up truck we would catch a hire car or a Corentyne bus: now me and my sisters piling in and fighting for the window seat.

Going for a drive on anything in wheels was the biggest treat imaginable. Hardly anybody had cars: the lawyers and dentists of course, and doctors in their Morris Oxfords. Oh and my big-shot cousins in Georgetown.

Off we would trundle through the streets of New Amsterdam, the Berbice River flashing past.

Past the mad-house and over Canje Bridge and up the Corentyne Highway where the country breeze sang in our faces bringing the smell of cane and cow dung and rice fields and paddy drying on wide expanses of hot concrete. We would stop for a cool drink at No. 19 Village or Palmyra, and Indian children would stand on the bridges over the trench and point at my hair and giggle *she lika gole hair dollee eh...*

We all loved the Williamsburg house, its faded pink paint and shutters beckoning us from the main road, over the bridge, into the front yard. We'd run through the shop and upstairs to the long gallery with its row of jalousie windows with the mesh keeping out the insects and letting in the breeze. Along the corridors and in and out of the bedrooms with the familiar mosquito nets looped up above, crawl under the beds playing the Uncle game, another story, where every night as a boy he would fall out of bed and roll underneath and Mummy woke him up and guided him back into bed and he never believe her next morning: "I didn't fall out of no bed, you telling lies on me!" And she said, "Yes you did." And he said, "No, I never." And one night Mummy decided to leave him there and when he woke up under the bed he sat up and rubbed his eyes and said, "What am I doing here?" Mummy laughed and laughed, saying "You believe me now?" So we played the Uncle game, rumpling up Mummy's old bed and rolling off the bed onto the floor taking turns who was going to be Uncle and who was going to be Mummy, "I never fall out of no bed" and "What am I doing here?" and "You believe me now?" sending us off in peals of laughter that brought Mother or Mummy running upstairs saying: "What's all this noise and commotion you-all making? (How children can make a game out of anything eh!)"

And slide I would slide into the doorway of Mother and Dad's room, all neat as a pin as they say, altar, mahogany chest of drawers, dressing table, big round mirror. Stand there peeping, ready to flee if I heard Daddy J's voice. There was the brass bed where Mother would harness Mummy's and Uncle's leg when they were small, whilst she went shopping. There, the window through which they would throw their toys. Against the wall, was that where the cot had stood? Was that where Evelyn, after crossing water, an unimaginable feat for ghosts, leaned over and picked up her baby Eloise, held her to her breast, Mother watching her from the bed?

Past the Bible room through to the kitchen with the jalousie window propped open with a stick and the blackened kerosene stove and the water barrel that another of Daddy J's sons had caused commotion with. Clattered down those back steps dented between 1937 and 1960 by the footsteps of a constant supply of half-children from both sides of the family...Charles and Henry (Doodoo) and Wallace and James and Lucille...carrying water, running into the back yard, past the pond, the coconut tree where Lucille had threatened to bash the head of Mummy's one and only doll.

When we stayed over, Desiree and I were allowed to help in the shop, weighing out sugar, flour, and rice from the great sacks on the floor, carefully positioning the cast-iron weights on the scales under Mother's watchful eyes, and the smiles and nods of her country folk customers.

The shelves were lined with tins of Carnation and condensed milk, Milo and Ovaltine, Vienna sausages, dried saltfish, mosquito coils and matches, packets of Kool-Aid, Red Rose tea, Marie biscuits, tablets of blue, Wrights Coal Tar soap, Lighthouse cigarettes, bottles of cough syrup, Limacol, jars of Vaseline, malt extract, castor oil, senna pods, Vicks

Vapour Rub...and in the refrigerator huge golden tins of New Zealand butter, hunks of Gouda and Edam, bottles of Banks' beer, ginger beer...

The customers called Mother by a variety of names... Mother, Mother Brazh, Aunty, Sister, Miss Angie, Mrs James, Gee...In and out of the shop they came, their hair and faces bearing trace memories of ancestors whose names and places of birth were all mixed up and pointed to the four corners of the earth.

As practically everywhere on the inhabited coast, only the original inhabitants were missing. From being early traders with the Dutch, then unwilling and incapable slaves, and runners for the British, the Amerindians, who were commonly referred to by the derogatory term 'Buck people', had withdrawn from the coast, melting into the interior.

Only when my grandparents moved up to Kwakwani were we aware of their presence, encountering them as they banked their canoes and walked up the track for a box of matches or a quart of cooking oil. Angie, with her fair skin and European history, knowledge of which was not or could not be handed down, the Catholic faith, her rosary, her big squashy bosoms and her belly laugh and her cigarettes and her inherited children and her vernacular punctuated with Creole and Portuguese and one or two indiscreet words that thrilled me no end, was as much part of this shop front gathering as were the women in saris and shalwars, or calf-length cotton dresses, fanning themselves with a roll of newspaper or a palm leaf, perspiration spreading under their armpits.

She spoke like a country woman, walked like a country woman, wore cotton dresses and big straw hats to keep out the sun. Leaned over the counter passing the time, her gold bangles pressing into her forearms. And I wasn't to know for a long-long time, what was the extra special thing she had, that had her name on the lips of countless country women who asked after her from behind their market stalls, or on the pavement outside New Amsterdam market as they waited for the Rose Hall bus, a long-long time after she left the Corentyne for Kwakwani.

Stupid as it may sound, I was eleven, in 1965, before I

realised that the old term 'coloured' applied to me. I remember the moment clear-clear. I was cycling down my street with my new friend BiBi. We'd been chatting about music, and BiBi asked if I liked the latest song from Motown in the American Hit Parade. "No," I said. Apart from Smokey Robinson I was more into the British pop scene, Herman's Hermits, The Dave Clark Five, Donovan, The Beatles, The Rolling Stones…I drew their mop-headed fringes all along the borders of my school exercise books, and wrote out phrases of the lyrics that particularly appealed to me, in a passion that washed over the hairs of my skin, throbbing through my fingertips.

"But why don't you like that kind of music when you're coloured?" BiBi's strange question surprised me so much I stopped pedalling and the bike wobbled.

"What?" I asked, puzzled. BiBi repeated the question, and I really didn't know what to say first. Different feelings rushed round in my mind. Anger at BiBi for being so foolish just because I didn't like one song, and anger too because over the past year music had become so important, was opening up such a new, exciting world for me; what did colour have to do with it? To think that BiBi actually saw colour in music and colour in me was stranger still. But it hit home somewhere else deeper; I knew full well my daddy was dark-skinned, as was all his family, but the whole of New Amsterdam appeared to be a rainbow of colours, one hundred tints of tan and brown and black and white and to the child I was then, that just seemed normal.

We knew little of Daddy's story. The Harrises came from the Berbice River; my Daddy, James Alexander Harris, was named after his father. His Mother, Mama, was Anna Rose Boyle. My Daddy was born in 1908, the youngest of eight boys and girls.

We knew our Daddy was an old Dad, more than twenty years older than our mother, and that all those aunts and uncles that dropped in from time to time were really our cousins, and that their children were our second cousins. All of them belonged to the English Church, apart from Aunt Marie, my father's Catholic sister, who lived in the self-same Pope St as the Church, and whose entrance every Sunday, caused us to look round, causing my mother to twist our faces back to face the front by our ears.

My own mother's family background was a cocktail, with the white-by-blood Hawkers and Brazhs and the black-by-partnership James.

In hindsight of course I would call myself naïve, but the clear-cut definition with which BiBi had identified me seemed entirely at odds with the terms that had so far been applied to me...'Blondie', 'Blue-eye dolly', 'white-skin girl', 'Potagee'.

From as far back as I could remember people were patting my head and commenting on my hair, my mother's girlfriends slipping their Cutexed fingers through those ringlets Mummy would style like Shirley Temple's with a comb dipped in water, fixing them at one side with a big ribbon bow; and every day without fail my mother 'pulled my nose' in an attempt to straighten it. Daddy's friends too sang *Pretty Blue Eyes* in the middle of their rum drinking and domino slapping, winking and laughing. And in those visits up the Corentyne, framed by the smell of cow dung and sugar-cane, small Indian children stared and giggled, pointing at my skin and eyes and hair. But BiBi prepared me for the contradictions that were to come my way, when there would be those who would wait for me at street corners and sing *whitey shitey penny a glass if you don't want it kiss me ass* and elders would advise *you mustn't shame your colour* and many suns and moons later in another life someone would call me a wog.

The story goes that Aunt Ena, Daddy's sister, a tight-lipped, brown-skinned woman with an energy as closely wound as a bobbin, would push me round New Amsterdam in my pram, boasting to all and sundry that *this baby, her brother's first-born, her skin is so fair because of course we had a white Barbadian in the family you know.*

Aunty lived right next door. She and Mummy didn't get on. Aunty was always "in and out of the house as if she owned it." Her quick footsteps could be heard cantering up the front steps and the front door pushed open without a knock or a "can I come in?" Instead it was, "Elizabeth, it's only me" and in she'd step, her lips barely framing the shape of her words before sentences sprang out. It was "Elizabeth, these children this" and "Elizabeth these children that."

Soon after Mummy got married 'Eloise' had become 'Elizabeth.' Daddy didn't like the name Eloise. He liked it even less when her half-brothers Wallace and Henry called her Sister Elo. So Elizabeth she became, and Liz. We were used to all that. Many Guyanese had a real name *and* a call name. Henry was called Doodoo. People protected their names from spirits, or protected their true-true spirit with a false name. Or maybe it was just left over from the practice of renaming slaves.

Aunt Ena's married name was Mrs White. Her husband had dead and gone a long time. We were frighten bad of Aunty. When we heard her footsteps, we would run and hide behind Mummy's skirts, or under the beds, wondering what we'd done now.

Of the many stories that tumbled out of Mummy's mouth on rainy days, the Tale of Mummy's Marriage to Daddy was a favourite. The Tale of the Circumstances of the Marriage was a close second to The Tale of Evelyn Dreaming Mummy. We would have been dragged in from the yard, or would have had enough of playing Ludo or Chinese Chequers indoors, and as night drew in and the crapauds began to croak, the fireflies to dance, and the bats begin to flutter in the eaves, ole higues and jumbies roamed about.

There wasn't much for children on the radio, and four of us cooped up needed to be entertained. We were paralysed with fright by tales of jumbies and ole higues...vampire women, balls of fire, in the branches of trees, waiting to suck the blood of babies. Yet we curled up on the floor by the rocking chair to hear such stories with anticipatory terror and delight, and from the night outside any small sound of bats or crapauds would have us screaming and scrambling onto the small lap of my mother.

But the home tales were a different sort, and no matter how many times we heard them, they were fresh each time. There was the tale of Lucille and the Doll, of Lucille Runs Away, Uncle Catches Typhoid, and James in the Tar Barrel. But the tale of The Circumstances of the Marriage began with Aunty.

Aunt Ena worked for the Singer Sewing Machine Company in Water Street. As well as selling sewing machines and parts, thread and needles and patterns, the business also offered a design, pattern-making, tutoring and dressmaking service. She was a seamstress at home too, and her sewing machine whizzed away when she came home, and posh white ladies trooped up and down her front steps.

All our clothes were hand-made; shop-bought clothes was a new thing, expensively hanging in the Georgetown department stores like Booker's and Fogarty's and Bettencourt's, all imported from the USA and Canada. Those clothes cost a hundred dollars, and the stroking of them was patrolled by toffee-nosed assistants who had pencilled eyebrows and long Cutexed nails. In any case, cloth was cheap, and anybody could get their yard and a half of satin or peau de soie, or seersucker, or chiffon, or cotton from Pitt Street or Gajraj Sawh, and take a magazine picture of Elizabeth Taylor wearing *the* dress and march into any number of dressmakers in New Amsterdam and say *you can make me that please?*

But Mrs White was a cut above the rest; the tilt of her nose told you that. She wasn't some Backdam dressmaker. She didn't sew for just anybody; real ladies were her clientèle...bank managers' wives, doctors' and lawyers' wives. My aunty was no housewife. She was a professional woman, British Guiana's new working class, fiercely protective of her journey and new status. From a childhood up the Berbice River she had come down to town, and worked her way up to her present situation, owning property in St John Street. She shared a house with Jim, her brother...*Captain* Harris, let me tell you, who worked for the Berbice Bauxite Company. His frequent work trips up to the interior saw him gone for days, even weeks at a time. Jim was a widower; he had lost his wife Adrienne in very unfortunate circumstances and was in need of a new wife.

From her position inside the window of the Singer Sewing Machine Company, Mrs White could see all the comings and goings. Who was going in the photography studio, who was coming out the Penguin Hotel, who was wearing one of her creations. Some people would fret her by blocking her view, leaning their bicycle on the railings outside, and she would tut and click her tongue and offer the sharp edge of it if a bicycle so much as touch the glass window.

One morning a donkey pulling a cart added to the traffic, slowing up the buses and cars, trotting, ears back, dreaming of the time he would be back in his little field nibbling clover. Mrs White was guiding the seam of Mrs C's new dress under her needle when she happened to look up and see a sight that intrigued her. A slim Portuguese girl crossing Water Street, coming straight into her establishment. She stopped midstitch. Is who in the Lord's name was that? She knew all the Portuguese families in New Amsterdam. Business people most of them. But she'd never seen this girl before. The door swung open and she came in, accompanied by an older Portuguese woman, hair under the Panama hat just turning silver.

"Good afternoon Madam..."

Wanting to learn sewing, I see.

The girl, fine as a string bean, had just finished Rose Hall High School, for Pete's sake. What she doing up the country?

Mr and Mrs J niece. From East Demerara. Lost her mother and father young. Brought up in the Corentyne. Doing Typing and Book-keeping. Oh yes.

She was amenable enough, a bit slow on the pattern cutting, but quick enough with a needle, to tack, hem, handle the sewing machine, thread it. Mrs White gathered the threads, created a pattern, began to weave.

There was her brother Jim, wifeless now for seven years. At forty-four, he didn't have one child to his name. Even his nieces and nephews coming and pass him now. But the choice in Berbice wasn't that great, and you have to move Up in life.

Look how she had to work her fingers to the bone, her eyes watering with all the straining to thread needles and hem.

She and Mr White never had the good fortune to have children so there was nobody to look out for her, except her niece who lived with her. Jim want the same thing to happen to him? Indian people had plenty family; nobody would be left to look after themselves when they were old. In any case they would move the whole family in, lock, stock and barrel.

She and Jim couldn't let that happen to the St John Street house what take blood, sweat and tears to purchase. But when you weed out those not planning to go abroad, not much was left. The coloured girls them were too lippy by half, and vain. The dark ones were wild and their hair not good; she didn't want the place stinking up with the smell of hot combs and burning hair. The light skin ones wanted a Portuguese boy who father had Business, or a white man. Fat chance! Those sons were destined for St Stanislaus College and business degrees in Toronto. But girls pushing for work now came knocking at the door here, trying to push their way in. Booker's and J.P. Santos had their full share. No, there wasn't any doubt at all. That girl looked ideal. Quiet, peaceable. Plus what were they going to do with her up in the country with all those rice and cane fields and sheep and cows?

We children would lie on the floor, fists propping up our chins. We were about to hear about the Quest and the Marriage.

Mummy had to be wooed and cajoled. She didn't want to get married to someone who was old enough to be her father. She wanted to carry on with her typing and her bookkeeping and maybe even get a job in town and board with somebody! Lord! That would be great! To have her own little key in her hand and step out to work! Not to have to ask anybody permission to go anywhere! She had grown into a good-looking girl and eyes were already following her. She'd still go to church, of course she would, she loved Our Lord more than life itself; had her own special rosary blessed by the Bishop, and was never happier than when kneeling in the church pew, head bent, eyes closed in prayer. But her upbringing had been so strict, Daddy J with his loud harsh voice and his leather belt, the wild cane...And plus, and plus...she really liked someone else, a Portuguese boy by the name of Patrick. Daddy J eye had lit on him that one time he came to visit, and since then she couldn't sneeze even.

Mummy had a habit of raising one eyebrow when she wasn't Telling All. No more details were forthcoming about Patrick. His name slipped into the ether like so many other lost names and fragments of stories, and didn't surface again until someone mentioned that he'd emigrated to Canada, and then, long long long time later, that he had died. In any case, we children were only interested in our Mummy marrying our Daddy, in looking at the photos of their wedding in 1953 and even with the naïvety of youth being struck by how much of a child our mother was, a slim dark-haired child, the spitting image of Evelyn, and Daddy, serious Daddy, looking as if he'd come to give her away.

But the wedding cause more trouble in the land of Job, as people used to say. Not only the story about how Mummy got licks bad from Daddy J before the wedding, but the moving in business too. This last Mummy had to be careful because there's only so much you could say to children, and as for the most part she got on all right with her in-laws, and didn't want to upset the apple cart. But after the wedding, which had to take place in the Anglican church for mysterious reasons, and after their honeymoon at 63 Beach, Mummy moved into the house at St John Street to find that Mrs White, her niece, and Daddy's mother Mama were still living there.

I am the only one of my sisters to remember Mama, remember her lying bed-ridden in the small back bedroom in Aunt Ena's house. She lay beneath the window which overlooked our front yard, her once-black hair silver. I have heard it said she had Amerindian blood in her. She too came from the Berbice River, had married my grandfather Harris and bore him eight sons and daughters. What were her thoughts as she lay there, hearing us whoop and cry, hearing car horns and bicycle bells, remembering her time, her children's time, the memories of plantations, the quiet lapping of the river on the sandbanks? Was the Amerindian connection true? I close my eyes and see the river, a clearing, an estate laid out in the manner they were with the big house and a massa and his lady and house servants scuttling. Then I see field slaves coming out at dusk beneath the tall columns of cane. Beyond the estate the jungle exists as it always had, its people melting into the mists. Time shifts and the slaves are free, the logies become family houses, people go walk bush, as they say. Somewhere a black man and an Amerindian woman make love.

"We didn't get on," Mummy would say of the family set-up she had married into. Aunt Ena and Daddy sat down at the dining table on a Friday night and did the household accounts together, something that they had been used to doing. But this made Mummy feel as if she was still a little girl, not a wife. To be true she still was a child, just seventeen years old, and believe it or not, seventeen is children age, and you only have to look at the photo to see that! But, child or not, is grow up she had to grow up, and that means responsibility.

One helluva commotion ensued, and Mummy ended up running away, back to the house in Williamsburg. This is where Daddy J became a hero, in my eyes at least, which is saying some because I am not ashamed to say that I did not like Daddy J one bit, not one bit! In the story my Daddy had followed his runaway bride and tried to persuade her to come home, but in his man-way never even asked her why she'd left, just demanded she come home and not shame him. She refused!

So down Daddy J came to New Amsterdam, whether by donkey cart, bus or hire car who knows? Down he came fuming with all the warring archangels at his shoulders. The man should have been a preacher, in fact he *was* a preacher, and that too is another story, but that voice had enough fire and brimstone in it to burn down the whole of St John Street: "You marry our Elo. She is your wife! On no condition, on no condition is she coming back until the house is cleared!"

In my imagination I saw him disperse Daddy's relatives as the Pharisees were dispersed from the temple, and disperse they did, although it was only to the house next door. And at last my Mummy had her own house, never mind the continuous to-ing and fro-ing between the two.

The song about the white Barbadian continued to be sung, especially as all the time I was growing up my blonde hair was bleached even more by the sun, and the blue eyes stayed blue. Mummy fumed at the ownership of this whiteness being attributed to some dead Bajan, although she noted Daddy's grey eyes and the range of light-skinned tones in Daddy's big family who, when they were all together, looked like the make-up range at Booker's cosmetic counter...Honey

Dust and Cinnamon, Bronzed Kiss and Deep Tan, Sundance Beauty.

Mummy wouldn't have acknowledged then that a seed of truth nestles at the root of all stories, and wouldn't have known that in the 1800s after slavery was abolished and the sugar industry all but collapsed, white Barbadians did immigrate to British Guiana looking for land and prospects that their small island couldn't offer them. She herself will say apologetically that she only went as far as the School Leaving Certificate.

As if to cement this link, just as people in the islands cement conch shells to concrete walls and garden steps, there on our Phillips radio sat a Barbadian conch shell as fat as a fool and a King.

Listening, listening, listening.

Mummy wouldn't have known about that because what they would have taught her in school, apart from Christianity, was that British Guiana was a colony and we had a King and Queen, and she and many young women would know the name of that King and Queen and their daughters, and the photographs of the new Queen Elizabeth and *her* growing family would occupy an equally prestigious place on the wall along with Jesus Knocking On The Door and a family portrait in sepia.

But Mummy's whole point about the Aunty business...and while we're about it we might as well call her Elizabeth lest she be remembered just as Mummy ...Elizabeth's whole point was that you didn't have to go digging that far back in the past to resurrect a white ancestor, for as plain as the nose on her face there was her own Daddy Cyril (God rest his soul) looking right down upon us from that photograph there and just one generation back. The presence of the photograph augmented and legitimised his existence in a way no half-baked story ever could.

And it would be way-way in the future before I would begin to wonder what my Daddy, as brownskin as brownskin come, may have felt about all of this, and the nose-straightening business, and whether Aunty (God rest her soul) ever had recourse to the thought that somewhere on the distant coast of Africa, there might have been an ancestor with skin as smooth and black as a tamarind seed, of whom she, they, might have been proud.

# 5

# Early Years

"Elizabeth! Elizabeth!"

My first memory is of falling through our gallery window, two storeys high. I was two-and-a-half years old. I still have the scar, half-moon shaped, an inch long on my left temple. The memory is as clear and bright as sunlight. I'd woken up from my afternoon nap, to hear the sound of children's voices from the flat downstairs. Mummy and my new baby sister Desiree were still asleep.

I pulled the little green rocking chair close to the window. There was laughter coming from the front yard. I put my elbows on the windowsill and leaned over.

"Elizabeth! Elizabeth!"

The girl from downstairs grinned up at me from the yard downstairs. She had the same name as my Mummy. She leaned back against the picket fence, her white teeth shining through the leaves of the Sourie tree. She began to play peepso with me and I began to laugh and stretch my belly over on the sill to see her better. My toes dangled on the rocking chair.

From the corner of my eye I could see a man walking down the street towards the back gate. He was wearing a Panama hat. Then I felt the rocker slip away and there was nothing under my feet but air, and all of a sudden the Sourie leaves were scratching my face and the world was upside down with the picket fence coming towards me. And the man's hat flies off and he is running running running towards me.

I can't remember him running up our front steps with me in his arms shouting "Mrs Harris! Mrs Harris!" or Mummy coming bleary-eyed to the door. I can't remember my cousin running over from next door, or being taken to New Amsterdam Hospital. Can't remember the panic or the screams, or blood pouring down my face or the stitches or the pain.

They told me all that later, like the fact that if the paling had stabbed me half an inch deeper in my temple I would have been dead-dead. I only remember the calling of the name *Elizabeth* and the falling.

I must have had a thing about windows. Not much longer after this, apparently I threw my puppy Rover out; luckily he lived to tell the tale.

Our gallery windows looked out over St John Street. Everybody called it the bend street because it didn't run straight like the others, but kinked halfway past Mrs Rosario's house then ran past half a dozen or so houses before it met Water Street. You couldn't see the river from here; Ramdehall's shop blocked it out. But look right and you could see the church spire of Our Lady Of Ascension, shining on Main Street. It was Mr Hartman from downstairs, the other Elizabeth's father, who had picked me up. He worked with Daddy on the tug as Chief Engineer. Sometimes I would lie on the floor of our living room and peep through the floorboards. I could see Mr Hartman with his feet stretched out, or Mrs Hartman doing her ironing. Mummy would slap my bottom hard if she caught me, telling me not to be so *fast*.

But Mummy couldn't catch me all the time. I *was* fast, would run away laughing, though Mummy's use of the word meant 'inquisitive' or 'nosey'. In any case, since the new baby came my days seemed longer, the world bigger; the windows and the front and back doors offered a world of sunshine, and it called me. I loved the feeling of the warm bare earth on my feet, the hot concrete; I dared myself to stand under the coconut tree in the back yard, craned my neck upwards, listened to the kiskadees calling their incessant *kiss kiss kiss kiskadee*, watched the ants run up the cherry tree, the lizards dart about on the fence. I hated to be called away. Lost in my own world of wonder, the name *Margrettte...!* didn't seem anything at all to do with me.

"You remember falling out the window, child? You have a good memory!"

We were gathered around Mummy in the gallery. The rain was falling so hard we couldn't go outside. Mummy was sitting in the rocking chair by the radio waiting for it to tell her the story of *Frenchman's Creek* by Daphne du Maurier.

Other times it would be 'Dr Paul', or 'Berbice Calling with Olga Sopes'. Our maid Ruby had gone home early, trying to miss the rain, leaving the house clean and smelling of polish. We'd begged and begged for a story and I'd started them off with my story of falling through the window.

"You have nine lives for true," Mummy said. "You know, I was fast asleep when I hear Mr Hartman banging on the door. 'Mrs Harris, Mrs Harris!' he was shouting. I got up and head for the door and there the man was holding my Margaret with blood pouring all down her face."

"I dint know it was Mr Hartman then," I said. "All I can remember is a man wearing a Panama hat like Daddy's." I rubbed the scar on my forehead, and my sisters crowded round to look, though all of them had seen it many times before.

"Tell us about my nine lives," I purr, happy that the limelight was on me, "and how you nearly dead with me." Desiree gave me a soulful look out of her big grey eyes. "You nearly kill we Mummy," she said. Elizabeth stopped rocking.

"O Lord, I have to go through that experience again!" she sighed. The three of us sat waiting expectantly. "You right, I nearly did dead with you. Hours and hours and still you weren't coming. The midwife was frighten I was going to lose you. I was sweating up the sheets, they mopping me with Limacol, poor Ruby running round like a headless chicken. In the end they had to send for Dr Ferdinand who said: 'This baby is a breech, she coming out foot first.'

"He tried to turn you but you wilful before you were even born. When you did come I didn't know a thing about it! I was in a daze! I didn't know I had a baby for four days! They said you didn't make a sound when you were born. Pim Pim! They didn't know if you were dead or alive. Dr Ferdinand had to slap you little bottom three four times before you utter a sound!"

We giggled.

"And you know," Elizabeth said slowly, "you nearly did die when you were nine days old. If it wasn't for Mother..."

We waited expectantly.

"I was only nineteen, you know, didn't know a thing about babies. Didn't know you had to wind them after a feed, before you put them down. It was like I was still in a trance too, I was still bed-bound since they gave you to me, you like a little dolly with a smooth mop of black hair…"

"Black?" Mary and Desiree stared at my hair.

"Jet black, like a cap. Her head small and round because she came out feet first…Well that morning I fed you and put you down and went back to sleep myself.

"The next thing I know, Mother was in the room shouting at me to wake up. She had you in her arms and was drawing milk out of your nose and mouth with her own mouth. You were choking. Mother said she'd come off the bus in Main Street and something sent her feet flying. She said her heart was in her mouth all the time she was in the bus coming, like she know something was wrong. She was praying for the bus to reach, and fly off by the church and pell mell down the street and sure enough there you were in your cot blue in the face and milk frothing out of your mouth.

"Praise the Lord, He send her in time. She ain name Angela for nothing you know. She's you guardian angel for true, some of them walking this earth for true-true. She was frighten bad you wouldn't live to see you nine day.

"She lost so many people…her sister Evelyn, her own mother Rosa just six months later, then my father. Wop wop, one after the other. Then she had to take care of so many of us! So she call you a blessing. Soon as she know you were a breech she said *this pickney gon walk!*"

"What she mean 'gon walk'? Did she mean when I walk out the house when I was three?"

Ah, another story.

I don't remember this at all which is strange as I was older, about three. But apparently I let myself out the front door, down the front steps, and out the gate. Over the gutter bridge and I headed up St John Street.

You'd think some neighbour might have seen me and shouted "Little Margaret, is where you going?" and chase my tail back home, kicking and screaming for so, for that's what neighbours did in those days, and parents would thank them for it; but no, not a soul saw me. In the heat of the day neighbours would be lying down themselves, snoozing or fanning themselves in a hammock under the bottom house. It wasn't the time of day for sweeping up the leaves with the pointer broom, or lifting the washing off the clothesline. Not the time of day for standing on the bridge idling. My head wouldn't have come up pass the top of anyone's fence. So I didn't just make it all the way up St John Street; but managed to cross Water Street.

How I didn't get knocked down I don't know, what with all those buses and bicycles and donkey carts and motor cars. No nosey parkers along here either, though they would be quick enough to spot me talking to boys a few years later and run to tell my parents and the world, faster than a jet plane streaks across the sky!

I wandered along the pavement pass the rumshop and the drunks, Ramdehall's grocery shop, the drug store, the Royal Bank of Canada. Bold as brass pass Wreford's General Store, J.P. Santos where you'd imagine I must have stopped to press my nose against the glass admiring all those new-fangled electric this and electric that, the shiny dolly furniture and big blue-eyed dollies. But I must have had business to mind. I bypassed all those distractions and headed straight for New Amsterdam market where the country buses pulled up. The market was underneath the Town Hall, a gracious-looking building made of wood and wrought iron, where not only could you pay your light bill or attend a concert in that fine auditorium where soon-soon I would find myself on stage, but you could look down from the elegant windows at passers-by and carry your eyes along the maelstrom that was Pitt Street.

In the cluttered gloom of the market below, traders sold everything, from cigarette lighters to plastic pens, and stall on stall was draped with clothes and provisions, kitchenware and linen. Bodies weaved past the butcher towards the sunshine, towards the river, where mothers rocked babies under parasols and displayed limes and coconuts, fresh hassa and mullet, live poultry and crabs on the ground.

Mrs Buddhu, Ruby's mother, was a market trader. Her stall was right at the front of the market forecourt, near to the bus stop. She sat there day in, day out, selling boiled sweets in the shape of fowl cocks, tamarind balls and sugar-cake, out of a large glass case. Half of her time, when not taking five or ten cents, was spent watching people come and go. Greeting Mrs This and Mr That. Doctor. Hello and Good Afternoon.

People crossing Water Street, people heading down Pitt Street, passengers off and on the yellow round-the-town-bus, the Corentyne buses. Passengers with their empty baskets, school-children with their lunch pails and school bags, passengers with their full baskets of bananas and yams and corilla, plantains and chickens and eddoes. Legs hauling themselves up the high step, legs with thread veins and Big Foot, feet in fancy white sandals from Bata, little white feet in plastic slippers...Mrs Buddhu did a double take. A little girl's legs were attempting to climb up the high steel step of the Skeldon bus. Mrs Buddhu's eyes travelled up the little figure, then glanced along the pavement. Wasn't that Mrs Harris's little girl? Mrs Harris must be going to see her mother...She looked left and right. No Mrs Harris. Quick as a mongoose she sprang up, nearly sending her fowl-cock sweets and tamarind balls and sugar-cake in their glass case flying, and sprinted across to the doorway of the bus where the driver was looking bewildered. She grabbed the little hand with the gold bangles.

"Mummy didn't even know I was gone!" I would complain, quoting what I'd heard time and time again. "She was too busy looking after *you*!" I would snarl at Desiree.

But then Elizabeth laughed, "Well maybe that is what your grandmother meant when she said you were going to walk!" Maybe I had been going to see my grandmother.

"I hate my name," I'd moan. "Why didn't you call me something nice?"

I'd glare at Desiree. *She* had a nice name.

"Don't say that," Elizabeth would scold, "it's a lovely name. You don't like Princess Margaret?"

"But you didn't name me for her!"

"No, you name after a British soldier's wife. But if you'd been a boy you would have been named after him, John, he was a nice soldier from the Highland Regiment. They came to sort the troubles out, you know, in '53. They travel on your daddy tug."

"Tell us about James and the tar barrel."

Elizabeth sighed and pushed the window open. The rain

had stopped and the smell of lilies and warm wet earth rose up. "Y'all haven't heard enough stories yet? Well this is the last one, y'all hear? I miss *Frenchman's Creek* now! Well y'know Brother Henry (Doodoo) and Wallace and James all live with us; a real house full! First we used to live at the back house way, way back off the main road when Daddy James used to work on the cane field and we had sheep and chickens and George the fowl-cock who was King of the yard...I was small-small there, so small when it rain the water was up to my belly and Daddy had to wade through and carry me on his back to the main road to go to school ...Well, we move from that house to the front house where Mother and Dad open up a shop...If Mother had been able to have her own children who knows where we all might have ended up? Albert and me probably in the convent with our poor sisters!"

"How come there are so many James's? Daddy J, and James our daddy, and tar-barrel James..."

Elizabeth shrugged. "Who knows? There are plenty Lucilles too. Your cousin Lucille, and my dear sister Lucille, God rest her soul ..."

"...and Aunty Lucille Mittelholzer, my godmother!" Des said, her thumb slipping out of her mouth for one moment.

"One night," Elizabeth began, "little James decided to play a trick on Daddy J..."

"How old were you?"

"Eight, nine...

"The Corentyne in 1943. War years. Shortages and unemployment. No street lighting. Dark nights and kerosene lamps. Shutters closed against the night, against the sandflies, against the mosquitoes. I remember the altars in my grandparents' house, the Bible, the ominous presence of my grandfather, the knowingness of him, his sharp ear. It wasn't jumbies that prowled outside. It was the presence of the Almighty, the fear of Him. Weary adults read Bibles, psalms and proverbs as mantras to themselves and their children, even as they registered the news that another merchant ship bringing flour and cooking oil was sunk by submarines in that black sea out there. And some of *our* boys were out there too, on the open sea and the skies even, and in that Europe, dying for the Motherland. And look these children here, all those hungry mouths waiting…

"Y'all know how strict Daddy James is…"

"Yes."

"James was always getting into trouble with Daddy. We didn't have electric light then, only candles and kerosene lamps. We used to keep a tar barrel in the kitchen for water. It was the boys' duty to keep it filled up from the vat downstairs. We didn't have running water then either…"

"How did y'all bathe then?"

"Bucket and calabash, not so different from y'all on a school morning when the shower too cold and you want bucket with warm water! You think Loretta mother does boil water for them? Y'all too too spoil."

"One night when we were supposed to be doing our homework and Daddy was reading his Bible, James decide to wait in the barrel and frighten Daddy. Your uncle and me had to pretend nothing was happening. James knew the barrel was empty, and that sometime Daddy would wander in the kitchen for something. You must remember that the place was pitch black, and the barrel was big enough to hold him, and by and by Daddy did go into the kitchen, and James was waiting…Is up James spring like a jack-in-the-box and up Daddy jump like his feet were on fire! All Daddy could see was two white eyeballs glowing in the dark! He drop his Bible and hold his heart, the barrel fall over braps! and James jump out rolling on the floor, holding his belly and killing himself with laugh. Me and your uncle were hiding in the doorway laughing so much we were crying! Tears were running down our face and our belly was hurting from laughing!"

Elizabeth had started laughing herself, at the memory, and set us giggling too as we watched her bent over, struggling to get the words out coherently, tears running down her cheeks.

"We laugh-*laugh!*…real bad, man…because nobody…ever get the better of Daddy James!"

Didn't I know this! I'd had my fair share of run-ins with him. A tall and forbidding figure, my grandfather. I'd never seen him smile, and it seemed he never missed an opportunity to shout "Young lady, what are you doing there!?" I was always jumpy in his presence, fearing the moment something would make him reach for the wild cane, or his belt. No-one dared answer him back or, God forbid, argue! 'But' could not be allowed to escape your lips. I could never forget that story Mummy had told us: how, just two days before her marriage, she'd been listening to the radio when Daddy J had shouted at her to turn it off. She'd just been about to go into the shower, and thinking he wouldn't hear her, she had whispered under her breath: "Two days and I'll have my own house and will listen to my own radio. Nobody will tell me what to do then!"

Unfortunately Daddy J's ears could hear a pin drop. Maybe it was his police training, sharpening the senses to catch anything the moment it manifested itself, who knows? He grabbed his belt and dragged her out of the shower. "You think you're a big woman? Getting you own house are you? Well take *this* and *this*! You washing you mouth on me? Well as long as you in this house you will obey *my* rules!"

I myself had borne the brunt of his discipline: had been chastised for singing along to the radio, for putting my hands on my hips, for idling. I was as scared of his voice as I was of his belt. Licks we were used to: the cane, the belt, the hairbrush, my daddy was scary enough...but Old James was twice as scary as my daddy. I could never tell my mother how much the fear of him was turning into hatred, because one of the most sacred of the ten commandments was the fourth, *Honour thy father and mother* which extended to grandparents, even grandparents by proxy.

The fear and the fact of this dislike, or hatred, was as strong as my fear of God, that fear that had been instilled in us for as long as I can remember. The fact of His being able to see into our hearts, read our *innermost thoughts* even. That's what had been drummed into us from as far back as I can remember; at home, in church, and in school. *He Sees All.*

Part of our weekly ritual was going to Confession every Saturday afternoon: cross Main Street, kneel in the back pew, wait for the mysterious cubicle at the back of the church to become free, releasing a cleansed soul in the shape of Mrs D or Mrs F, who would return to an empty pew and bury their heads in their hands, their lips moving silently as they underwent their penance. Each Saturday afternoon, I ran through the list of my perceived sins as I waited my turn to enter that cubicle with the dark curtains and the meshwork trellis that was supposed to disguise the priest within; even the tone of his voice took on a conspiratorial whisper.

I would search my soul for the things I had done wrong that week...pinched Desiree because she told a lie on me, stole Mary's teething powder because I liked the taste, answered Mummy back with a *but* because Daddy wasn't there.

Fear drove me in there, fear reminded me that I had to tell the truth because He, God, knew it anyway, there was no point in lying about the pinching or the stealing or the bad thoughts about your mother. And even though you could guess which priest was sitting in the dark, and you knew he could see it was you, part of you felt you were in the presence of God Himself; didn't they tell us that these priests were God's representatives on earth? And out they would tumble, my clumsy words, and you could hear the priest nodding, making judgement, and there was no joy like the joy of receiving your penance, your absolution, for the weight of it determined just how bad you'd been, and in order to get back into God's good books you received the sentence of three or more Hail Marys and an Our Father with bliss.

There was nothing like that feeling of being made whole and clean as you walked back to the pew, bowed your head, did your penance, and, liberated, walked out into the sunshine, God's child again. Mummy received her wonderful daughter again, who climbed up the front steps with a smile and offered to change the baby's diaper, clear the table, close the windows for the night, without even being asked.

Try as I might, and pray as I might, I could not include Daddy J in the search for forgiveness, apart from coming to my own conclusions that my dislike was a mortal sin, which I placed deep down in my dark soul, and brought out the venial sins one by one to compensate. I could neither articulate nor utter the feelings he initiated in me, and it wasn't long before I realised that, worse than the fear I had of him and the punishments he eked out, was the fact that *he made me feel as if I was a bad person.*

But Mummy was coming to the end of her story, relaying how poor tar-barrel James had more than paid for his little prank with a sound thrashing from the infamous leather belt, and Mummy and Uncle got their share too, for being *complicit*. And the talk then, of our grandparents' imminent move from Williamsburg to Kwakwani, some hundred miles up the Berbice River, gave me a lift at the thought that Daddy J and his belt were going to be so far away, but at the same time, my spirits sank, realising that of course, Mother would go too, lovely Mother, with her big squashy bosoms and lap, her silvering hair, and bellyful laugh, the curl of the Lighthouse cigarette from between her fingers. "Daddy, lef the pickney them alone," she would chide her husband, who carried his anger at the world like a twenty-foot cutlass. "Run away and play, walk far girl." And the Williamsburg house with its double-front doors, the shop with the long wooden counter, its shelves of evaporated milk and New Zealand butter, the long gallery upstairs where Des and I would chase each other and the back yard of fruit trees with the memory of Charles under the mango tree, would slide out of our family's hands with the exchange of florins and shillings, guineas and dollars, cents and a paper cheque from the Royal Bank of Canada.

In one of the early pictures they took of me I am standing in our street, wearing Wellington boots and holding a roll of paper in my arms. Whose camera was it, I wonder? Photography was an expensive business. People went to the Photographer's Studio, dressed to the nines, walked with a hairbrush, used the mirror in Mr Bacchus's studio with the backdrop of foliage on the walls...if anybody had their own camera, it meant they were rich, man!

I can't remember anybody owning a camera in our house, just like we never had a telephone, or a modern record-player; so it must have been one of those rich uncles up from Georgetown on a visit to the country cousins...Anyway, there

I am coming home from Bowling's Nursery School which just up the top of our road. I'm carrying some first masterpiece no doubt. That picture tells you something about our road, because the pot-holes were always something to complain about, by cyclists or taxi drivers, or those lawyers in their Morris Oxfords. You can see the road wasn't paved yet; everything look a little rough, eh? Dirt road, picket fences all up the road, the wooden bridges over the gutter. You can see the road curving round by the solitary lamp-post, where the Rosarios used to live, till right at the end it disappears into Water Street.

My second real memory was a dreamtime one. I don't know how else to describe it because I was both asleep and awake. I was small-small, maybe even so small it preceded the memory of falling out the window, but because *that* one was so vivid and dramatic, and corroborated by the scar and the memories of others, this one took a quiet second place.

I'd been asleep and was stirring. The afternoon heat had me perspiring all along my forehead and the back of my neck, where my curls lay damp, and between those folds where mothers would pat talcum powder...the tops of our thighs, the backs of our knees.

My toddler limbs dangled over the cane seat of the Berbice chair, and I could feel the pattern indenting little circles, like ten cent pieces, on the backs of my thighs. My eyes were struggling to open themselves; light and shadows were dancing through the thin skin, like it does on water, and there was a faint chattering, a singsong of voices. But sleep still wanted to hold me down, pin me close in his embrace, keep my arms in a vice, caress the rise and fall of my belly.

I had a strong sense of a visitor in the room, of someone who was getting ready to leave. I could hear the repeated words of farewell, those long preparations that make slow passage to the front door. And I could hear my mother crying.

The visitor had a lilting voice; light, yet lively, and her perfume was different from the one that Mummy used. The scent had settled strongly over the room and hung in the air, through the taste of my breathing and the torpor through which I dozed. I remember willing my eyes to open, wanting to be conscious, wanting to see who it was, but my eyelids refused, and my fingers fell back against the chair uselessly.

"You want me to wake her?" I heard Mummy ask.

But the lady with the perfume said "No, No" and came closer and planted a soft kiss on my cheeks, a brief kiss, silky with lipstick. A cool breeze took her place and she was gone.

The lilt of their voices, the taste of her tears, the sound of Mummy sobbing and Daddy saying, "Now, Now..." all moved away and became distant; there were footsteps going down the front steps, the catch of the gate, the beep of a car horn.

That was the moment sleep decided to leave too, slide out of my body and go, taking the light with him, and the shadows. When I did manage to open my eyes the room was dark and I was all alone.

"She will sleep through an earthquake," Daddy said once. No, twice.

Whatever year that was, my bed was shaking to hell and I was enjoying the ride. I nestled into my pillow and from far away heard Daddy's voice.

"We should wake her," my mother said, from far away.

When I woke up it was morning, and there was the evidence: the cracked streets, the broken fence post, the split drainpipes.

"Where were YOU when the earthquake shook?" the headlines in the newspapers asked.

Was it you, Lucille, who interrupted my sleep?

The faces of women with dark hair emerge from the tip of my pencil. From nowhere has come this urge to draw, imprint patterns and swirling lines, the faces of exquisite women, wings, the branches of trees. Paper has to be found for me, half-used notebooks, the backs of envelopes, discreetly stolen pages from the Household Accounts Books. I would dream of that pen and pencil set from Booker's, with matching notebook. Five dollars! Daddy shook his head.

# 6

# Lucille

After their father Cyril and their mother Palmyra died, my mother's half-sisters, Sybil and Ismay, had been sent to live in a convent in Demerara, and their brother Compton to their uncle, Palmyra's brother. Their sister Lucille would become one of the Williamsburg brood, coming to join my mother and her brother and Daddy J's sons, Henry, Wallace and James.

I could not conceive of having to live in a convent. It was bad enough being a day-pupil, with the nuns like dark-shrouded ghosts gliding along the corridors ready with ruler and cane, sharp eye and whiplash tongues.

But the story of Lucille echoed that of Evelyn's, and my ear stole it from the mouth of Elizabeth, my mind and pen drawing on and embellishing another beautiful tragedy. Even the name of Lucille's mother was beautiful. Palmyra. There was a Palmyra village up the Corentyne, with a small perfect Catholic church just off the main road where the New Amsterdam priests would travel up and say mass once a week.

Lucille's story had all the right ingredients: haunting names, lost and adoptive parents, and a wild and beautiful heroine.

Elizabeth didn't like to talk about this sister; it made her sad. But again and again I would prise out bits of her story, which fell like chips of walnut out of the shell.

"I only had one dolly," Elizabeth would say, "and Lucille threatened to bash her head in on the coconut tree, or throw her in the pond."

I remember this comment when I pause at the door of my mother's bedroom, where a wealth of reproduction dolls, Victorian, Edwardian, baby dolls, dolls with ringlets and bonnets, white lace dresses and soft buttoned shoes, recline on her bed and stare down glass-eyed from the chest of drawers. And I would remember my sisters and me, our own childhood. At no time did we ever have more than four dolls between us.

"I'm keeping them for the grandchildren," she says, and counts them off on her fingers: "That one's for Aimee, that one for Kanisia, that one for Chloe, that one…"

But I know it's more than that.

Despite the discipline, despite the combination of Daddy J's glowering presence, the Bible, the belt and the cane, I can imagine the ruckus in that Corentyne household between the disparate children. Children fighting for their own level, white-skinned, black-skinned, living and going to school amongst a mostly East Indian population at Rose Hall Village.

One can imagine fights between the boys, between the girls, small and varying jealousies. Lucille, some few years older than Eloise, was a fire-brand. Maybe this was what held my attention; I myself had begun to attract descriptions which for the most part confused me: in addition to the *she lika dolly eh* came *devil chile*, most times in jest, from the sailors Daddy worked with and who would often drop in to share a bottle of rum. *Fiery nature. Plaster for every sore* was another, describing my way of having good excuses for everything. *Daydreamer* was often used, many times with a shake of the head.

I was developing an ability to fill in the gaps between stories that were not fully told, my imagination lifting off like dreams of flying. Some characters became larger in the telling, their presence growing in visual and dramatic imagery, silences become as bright as stained-glass windows. So I can see Lucille Hawker clear as day, walking to Rose Hall High School in the forties, her black hair swinging, her half-Portuguese, half-Scottish skin bronzed in the noon-time sun. I hear the other girls hissing *'whitey shitey'* as she passes, see them swing their satchels against the backs of her knees, girls jealous of her high head and her movie star looks.

Boys, you see, don't do bitching. They just want to ogle, fight, conquer and eat. Like peacocks they saunter along the pavement making jewelled feathers out of words: *Hey Honey, Evening Star, Rainbow of Rose Hall, Hey Movie Star girl*…Their words are as hopeful and bold as those names inscribed on the sides of buses...*Lady Godiva, Sweet Dreams, Princess Bountiful*. The peahens, dull and brown, kick pellets into the dust of Lucille's shoes.

The peacocks called and called, as they do, rivalling the cockerels' chorus, taking over from them mid-morning, puncturing those Angelus and lunch-pail lunch-times with their common lord-like manner.

Calls louder than the call to prayer from the mosque, taller and brighter than the flags of the temple. They reach the ear of Daddy James chastising Lucille in the yard.

"Tie back your hair! Button your shirt! Go help mother in the shop!"

Her tears wash the back steps; her fingernail breaks on the scrubbing brush. One peacock called even louder than the others, louder than the Roman Catholic church bell, than the sigh of the Standard English exercise book, than Mother grating coconut on the kitchen table; louder even than Daddy J's voice. The peacock shape-shifts and becomes a steed, twenty hands high and wide mane flying. He rides right up to the drawbridge, clatters over the drain with his love letters and anxious brave heart. Lucille's fourteen-year-old face from the gallery window fuels him, puts fire in his belly and a sword in his tongue, and she runs downstairs with all of the Trade Winds behind her, kicking the exercise book to Kingdom Come.

British Guiana was used to runaways. Time was they used Amerindians as trackers to fetch back black boys tired of kissing ass. But those days were done; besides, memory was not that short that there wouldn't be those who wouldn't raise their eyebrows at a *black man* going pell mell to fetch back some white girl, because believe me or not, white means white when it matters to some, Portuguese or not.

So the Corentyne Highway, pot-holes and all, gives her smooth passage, the movie star girl, and from New Amsterdam stelling the ferry carries her across the Berbice River to Rosignol, then the steam train takes up the relay, puffing across the Mahaicony Bridge and back home to Buxton.

Back in Williamsburg Daddy J roared with the intensity of a hurricane. His words plummeted down on the tops of the heads of Angela, Eloise, Albert, Henry, Wallace and James, whose eyes were all filled with the loss of their sister. "That girl will never set foot in this house again."

My mother shakes her head.

"She left us in church, Albert and me, whilst she made her getaway."

And stories filtered back up the country. "I saw Lucille dancing in the streets of Georgetown. People were dropping money in a hat"; "Lucille living back in de Buxton house, God know what she eating."

She was fourteen years old.

Now, Guyana's main airport is called The Cheddi Jagan Airport. In my time it was called Timehri, an Amerindian name adopted to symbolise a new, united, independent Guyana. Before that it was called Atkinson Field, or simply the Base, built during the war by Americans and named after its Major. I would have my own time to mingle socially there, at motor sport events, and an unforgettable occasion in 1978 when I partied and sighed at the sight of handsome Cubans, paid for direly at the end of the evening as the car I was in turned over at the side of the road. But this is Lucille's story, and that's how my rebellious aunt was to meet her man, an American called Johnny.

Next thing anybody know, plane ticket buy and they gone. Away she flew, my beautiful aunt, she had set her sights way up there in the sky and across the ocean. Country life was not fuh she. Angela cried, Eloise cried. Nobody knows if the boys cried. But in she tripped one hot afternoon, into our house in St John Street. Come to see her sister Eloise and her baby girl. Soft oily lipstick on my baby cheek, that perfume, that lilting voice I know now was an American twang, high heels down the stairs.

"No," Elizabeth tells me firmly, over and over. "No, no. Lucille was gone long before you were born. And she never came back. You must have been dreaming, or it was somebody else."

In her photographs, taken in the United States, she could be Elizabeth: same dark wavy hair and features, slim and elegant, posing by an American front door, on the bonnet of an American car, another nestling close to her husband Johnny, headscarf Hollywood-style, an Ava Gardner look-alike. Was that the car that killed her that day on an American Highway? No, it was cancer, someone said. Get the story right.

# 7

# Sisters

Desiree put a spanner in my works. Before she came along I was the golden-spoon, the spoil child, the Bajan reincarnation, the dolly to dress up in pink polka-dot chiffon and springy can-can, waist sash with big ribbon-bow. It was I who got tickled under the chin, stroked and petted, thrown up in the air and settled amongst white embroidery anglaise in the big black perambulator. Rhett Butler himself could not be prouder than my Daddy.

Relations queued up to cut my tiny fingernails, change my diaper, fasten the ribbon-bow to the fat curl that hung over my right ear. Aunty Carmelita, Daddy's niece, childless herself, played peepso with me through her fingers, waved at me from Aunt Ena's house, came clambering up our front steps hot breath and chubby-cheeked to play with me.

She fought with Elizabeth to bathe, powder and dress me in my shimmy, to slip my baby feet into soft white satin shoes, to take me for pram rides to the Botanical Gardens. Aunty Carmelita would sing of the babies she was planning to have with her lovely Beau. Cowboy Uncle Beau, I would come to think of him, in his cowboy hat and long legs in blue jeans and blue-blue eyes in a nut-brown face.

Then Desiree came along in 1956. Gone was Mummy's lap. Gone was the soothing creak of the rocking chair on the polished floor, Mummy's bosom and Mummy's singing. My thumb became my comforter, and the threads of soft cotton which I plucked with my right hand. Instead, "Go and play," Mummy said, as she lifted the new baby under her brassière. And "Ssshh! The baby sleeping!" as I rolled Duckie Wuckie over the floorboards.

This new baby was darker than me, had dark curls that would stay dark, that Elizabeth would rub oil into and plait into pigtails, adorn with ribbon-bows. She had big grey eyes like Daddy's, and soon let everyone know that she was Mummy's Girl.

She became a part of Mummy's shoulder, Mummy's arms, and Mummy's hips. She held Mummy's attention so that they slept tight most afternoons, like the time I fell out the window, and the time I went walkabout to catch the Skeldon bus. And nobody had even missed me.

When Desiree eventually learnt to crawl, she used her knees to crawl after Mummy, wanting lap, snuggle, kiss, cuddle. When she found her legs it was to run after Mummy and bury her face into her skirts. She cry-cry, cry-cry, pointing her finger at me. Maybe I pinched her sometimes.

We both sucked our thumbs until the age of eleven, and for fifty per cent of our growing-up years she and I would fight, fight, fight, and practise our ever-growing knowledge of the art of sarcasm, cynicism, irony, and disdain. The other fifty per cent was spent sharing dolls and boyfriends.

In the yard downstairs she dared to demand my doodoo, my much-loved tricycle, wailing "Mummeee!" at the very top of her voice for the slightest thing.

"Is mine!" I would say, gripping the handlebars tight and curling my toes over the pedals.

"Give your sister a go," Mummy would peacemake, "she smaller than you."

"Is mine!" I would repeat, "she got *her* dolly."

And I'd pedal away furiously across the concrete. Desiree's piercing scream would rise up over the top of the swing, over the coconut tree and through Aunty's window next door.

"Elizabeth," would come the call, "Elizabeth! What are you doing to that child!"

"Margaret! Margaret! Bring your little tail right this minute before I tan your hide!" And I'd be so angry I'd kick that trike over, leaving its wheels spinning on the concrete.

"I born first," I would say, as she trailed behind me, wanting to play. "I get for choose." I planted the doll on the bottom step, deciding, "Matilda is going shopping."

"Chuch," Desiree says. She has Elizabeth's old mantilla in her hand and drapes it over the doll's springy blonde curls. Its marble eyes gleam through the holes.

"Boo eye," Desiree says, "Mahgit eyes. Dohee eyes." She pushes her face close up to me and stares unblinkingly through spider-leg lashes. Her cheeks are still tear-stained and there is mud on her nose. I stare back, skinning my eyes wide. I wasn't going to blink first.

"You got dirty-water eyes," she states. "Rain-falling eyes."

"Haven't."

"Have."

"Haven't."

"Have."

I blink, and pinch her. She opens her mouth to bawl, the M-word starting to form on her lips. I mimick her, forming the Mummy-word silently. Desiree's lips tremble.

"Don't jare me." She sniffs, then sticks out her tongue, pink from Kool-aid. "Top tay nasty ting bout me."

"Top tay nasty ting bout me," I *jeer* her.

The grey eyes begin to mist up again.

"Matilda going to Wreford," I decide, lifting the mantilla off the doll. I wedge one of Elizabeth's old purses under the doll's stiff arm. "We need a new tape measure and a spool of cotton thread to make we new church dress."

Desiree smiles triumphantly. "Tilda go chuch."

"You are Daddy's girl," Elizabeth told me time and time again. "You only listen to him anyway."

Daddy bleeds out of my memories.

We would walk to take the breeze in the cool of the afternoon when he was home from the river. He held my hand whilst Elizabeth pushed the pram along the stelling or up to the Botanical Gardens. I had got used to Daddy not being home half the time. Many mornings I would wake and he wouldn't be there. Evenings later there would be the sound of the motorbike and "Anybody home?" from downstairs. He would wheel his motorbike in the yard and climb up the front steps to "Daddy!" "Daddy!" "Jim?"

He fell off that bike once, on the road to Everton. Probably skidded on the edge of a pot-hole or to miss a fowl-cock. Ended up in New Amsterdam Hospital and we went to visit him with a dish of food and there he was with his leg cocked up in plaster and bruises up and down his arm.

And other times Mummy got a ride or two, sitting side-saddle like Cyd Charisse or Audrey Hepburn in *Roman*

*Holiday* or some film like that, disappearing up St John Street pot-hole road, her hands gripping Daddy waist and her sling back feet curling over the pedals.

On those walk out afternoons with Aunty This and Uncle That or Mrs So-and-So leaning over the pram or running coarse hands on my head saying, "Man Jimbo man you got a nice family here you lucky so-and-so," and "How come you got all the luck Captain, even you wife looks like one of you daughter," my Daddy and 'young enough to be his daughter' Mummy laughed and would touch hands and hats would be tipped before we would move on again to window shop along Water Street. Pass the rumshop door open wide and calypso wicked music bursting out and the pram rolled past fast, Mummy step quick-quick while my Daddy raise his hand greeting, "Who is that, some no-good who lef his wife at home?!" And when time rolled on and there were four of us the same compliments would come and my Daddy thought nothing of exploiting that Jerry Lewis joke, "I got four daughters, all girls."

Afternoon bleeds into evening. We're going to something called Coney Island. The flat-land by the river opposite the Gardens is full of light and movement. Carousels whirl and horses dance, popcorn and candyfloss crackle and spin, peanuts glow out of glass cabinets, hot spits of fire flash upwards, the sides of lorries shift and figures playing organ music move mechanical arms up and down. I'm dazzled by the light and the music and the night. I hold Daddy's hands tight-tight, neck craning backwards to look up into the night sky which is full of fairy lights and a giant wheel spinning round slow-slow with basket chairs swinging perilously from it, and as we watch, people climb in and are whisked away and upwards.

"You want to come?" Daddy's voice is close to my ear.

I hold back, frightened, against Mummy's skirts. "No, No!"

Daddy loosens my hands from his and I watch him walk away and fold his legs into the basket which swings him away in the giant wheel machine away and up, up, up. I start to cry but not because I am afraid but because I have changed my mind.

"I want to go now, I want to go now! Daddy, come back!"

The sky swallows him up and I am filled with the pain of falling, just like the time I fell out of the window, only this time the ground is up there where my Daddy is and he is the one who is upside down and falling away and away and away into the night sky.

Mary was a roly-poly baby. Her belly was round and fat from Carnation milk.
"This baby can't stomach anything else," Elizabeth tells Carmelita. "Not breast milk, cow's milk, Cow & Gate, not Nestlé!"
"Never mind, Liz." Carmelita's eyes are huge and brown like Mary's. She holds the little fat fingers close to her own cheek, which is not as chubby as I remember. "Is a baby, nuh?" She runs her hands over our new baby's dark springy curls as Elizabeth rocks Mary close.
"You're the first baby to match my eyes," my mother sings, "not like those cat eye girls there."
"Is who eyes I got then?" I ask. "Is not fair, you and Mary match. Des and Daddy match! Who match me?"
"Don't you know?" Elizabeth laughs at me, at my pouting lips. "I find you under a coconut tree!"
"Me and Daddy got gey eyes," Desiree chirps. "Gey eyes." She hiccups.

Daddy's sitting on the porch with his Banks' Beer looking down at us in the front yard. We're fighting over the swing. He'd made it himself, knocked it up from his carpentry corner under the house by the septic tank. Five nice planks of greenheart wood. Two length of ship's chain from work. Room for all three of them and they still fighting. My mother is pushing us to the rhythm of her voice.
"Settle you bottom down Mary, that's it, hold on tight now! Tight to the chain like that. Up, up and away, fly little dumplin, up you go! Butterfly can't touch you, marabunta can't catch you, bee can't sting you, dove and pigeon fly out the way!"
Then is Desiree's turn and she want Mummy to push her

too, she want Mummy to sing 'Fly little dumplin' too. She squeals, her pigtails and ribbon bows flying back and forth, slapping against her cheeks.

Then I slip onto the wooden seat, nose turned up just like in that baby picture somebody took on Tita's doorstep. I don't want nobody to push me; I am not a baby. I dig my feet into the ground and push off, skinny arms working the chain, sending myself as high as the bougainvillea bush.

"Margaret, be careful!" my Mummy shouts. "You want to break you tail? Jimbo, you see the madness in this girl?"

Jimbo laughs. I am not listening to anybody. I am lost in the blue of the sky as it comes closer and closer. The breeze blows past my ears just like it does when we're driving up the Corentyne, and my head is hanging out the window of the bus or the pick-up truck, not quite believing that breeze can cut so sharp even though everybody say "Berbice breeze sharp bad man." But you, Margaret Harris, never listen and who don't hear must feel, and of course I come flying off the swing, rubber slippers freefalling, knees skinned, big toe splitting wide open on the concrete post.

My 'wilfulness' is beginning to become apparent. I am 'hard-ears', I am even being referred to as 'the devil child'. And where did this begin? Ah! there is the Tale of Aunty, Me, and the Bank Manager's Wife.

The Wife of the Manager of the Royal Bank of Canada was one of Aunty's clients. She came for a fitting one day, and Aunty called me over. I must have been about three or so.

"Say Good Afternoon to Mrs..." Aunty said.

"What a darling child," the lady was reported to have said, and leaned down to kiss me.

But I was beginning to dislike the faces of adults looming over me. Women's face-powdered cheeks and sickly scents, the spreading of perspiration under their armpits, the slick of lipstick left on my cheeks.

So I turned around, and cocked my bottom up to the face of the Wife of the Manager of the Royal Bank of Canada.

Now cocking up your bottom at Carnival is fine, if you're old enough and wild enough, but not from a golden-haired daughter of Captain Harris, not from the niece of Mrs White, seamstress.

Aunty's temper erupted, her face a picture. Blood vessels palpitated, guttural sounds not heard since the dawn of language escaped her throat. The enormity of her shame was legendary.

Licks? Course I got licks! You didn't spare the rod and spoil the child!

And although the story acquired a comedic twist in the years that followed, there remained dismay in the recognition that the devil incarnates in the most innocent-looking of children.

# 8

# New Amsterdam Story

This is what we knew: our bare footsteps padding across the dark polished floorboards, the square-armed Morris suite in blue leatherette, the Berbice Chair, the playroom in the gallery Daddy had fenced off with the little green gate. The rocking chair by the radio; Mummy sitting there, listening to Radio Demerara. The conch shell we were told came from Barbados, smug on top of the radio on a white doily, listening to stories that came from the islands. Him and the radio both thought they were King.

The tall windows in the gallery looked out over that same Sourie tree that had staggered my fall; her spirit had angled me so the paling fence only sliced my temple sideways. I talk to her sometimes, and gather her fruit thankfully, eat them green with pepper and salt.

The sunlight on the gallery floorboards ran into the bedrooms across brass and wooden beds, mosquito nets hanging like old wedding dresses, Mummy's mahogany dressing table, the white lace doilies, wooden-handled hair brushes, Pond's cold cream, Blue Grass cologne, dusting powder, silver baby-comb and brush set.

The medicine cabinet on the wall displayed a large bottle of mercurochrome for grazed knees and elbows, a fat wad of cotton wool, sticking plasters, Limacol and Phensic for Mummy's headaches, Vicks Vapour Rub, and silver envelopes of baby teething powder.

We stole the teething powder whenever we could. Unwrapped the silver carefully and dipped our fingers in. Touched it to our tongue.

Was trouble for so when the baby was crying and no teething powder left.

Two slap and a warning about thieves and how God watching and hearing everything you do.

Hanging on the outside wall between the two windows in our parents' room was a new fandangled pulley washing line, because *downstairs line always full man, these children run through clothes like water*.

I would become the proud owner of the gallery bedroom (unless we had visitors) by order of being the oldest, whilst my sisters had to share the back bedroom, with that ole higue dounze tree creaking and scratching on the window all night. No longer would I be disturbed in the middle of the night as one or other of my sisters climbed over deep-sleep bodies to wee-wee in the potty under the bed. I crept into my sacred sanctum like an Egyptian Queen, had my own altar complete with crucifix and Infant Jesus of Prague and my own plastic pink hanging wardrobe. Different clothes would soon swing there, mini-dresses and bell-bottom trousers, chain belts. I had to put up with Mummy's sewing machine by the side window but didn't mind as I was learning to sew my doll's dresses. I could pull the louvre door to, between my parent's bedroom and mine, shut the other door that opened into the gallery, and could spread myself across my own bed without fighting arms and legs all night. But come Masquerade Night, when the procession and the beating drums and frighten-face men in costume came running up the front steps and men with sticks pulled faces at children and danced in the middle of the street and Aunt Sally pushed her wooden head through my bedroom window, I would fly fast to nestle up between my sisters, a tangle of arms and legs hiding under the sheets.

At other times I grudgingly gave up my little kingdom to visiting relatives, Uncle Compton, Doodoo, Wallace...and on one occasion cried so hard my Aunt Joyce said, "O Lord! Me and your uncle will sleep on the Morris chair!" But Daddy's eyes and voice and his fingers itching on his belt shut me up quicktime.

Evidence of Daddy's carpentry was everywhere: the green baby rocker I'd stood on before I plummeted out of the window; the shelved partition between the hall and the dining room shelves which held the crockery and served as a bar where the rum punch was swizzled; the tall built-in glass cabinet storing the best glasses, the ice-cream dishes and the curly pink salad dish. The fridge purred in the corner by the window, always stocked with a jug of boiled water, Kool-Aid or home-made lemonade, left-over food, and fresh cow's milk, bought earlier that morning from bow-legged Channa, who'd come cycling up the street, milk churns and weighing jugs swinging from his bicycle handles.

The cats...Toots and Cooks and Smokey and Mitch... rubbed up against your legs in the passageway, leading you to the kitchen past the cooler with the lattice window propped open, bread under the fly mesh, the cookie jar. Past the bathroom and its concrete floor, the shower head where the spiders dangled (as did a strange enamel implement with rubber tubing hanging from a hook). Into the kitchen with the old mangle and the washing machine, the easy chair, the table where meat was chopped and flour was rolled, the blackened kerosene stove, the side window through which you could see Aunty's house squatting under the coconut tree; the sink where Mummy stood washing dishes, her skirts full enough to hide beneath, the guava tree constantly rapping on the window. Ruby, and later Baby, washed crabs fresh from the market in that sink, before plunging them into a pan of boiling water.

The back door was always open, except when it rained, the dounze tree pushing and spreading herself over the porch, bending nosey over the neighbours' yards and the gutter where dirty water, dead leaves, rotten guavas, genips, dead crapauds and cherryade tops floated and gurgled along. One of our puppies died on this porch, tied up on the railing; he slipped off one night and was hanged by his lead. I shudder to think of him struggling to claw his way back up, his little body swinging when everybody was asleep.

On these back steps on a Friday, Indian Betty descaled the fish, her apron skirt through her knees, basket full of mullet and shrimps, and sometimes hassa, their heads and moist eyes turned towards her. She smelt of the sea; silver scales fell from her knife on to the back-step, down on the yard below, where the cats circled. She would fillet the fish, cutting the heads off and discarding them, laughing because one thing my mother couldn't stand was to look at the head of a dead fish. If anybody wanted to frighten Mummy, chase her round the house with a fish head!

When Betty stood up, she became more than a fish woman;

she became graceful, her strong arms positioning the basket on the coil of cloth on her head, and off she went, undulating and sashaying along St John Street, fishwife mouth hollering "Feessh! Get yuh fresh feessh!"

Under the bottom-house was Daddy's carpentry corner in the unfortunate position by the septic tank. Every few months the council truck moved slowly down the street and stretched its thick black tube into the yard. It was an occasion for us to swing on the gate, watching with morbid fascination as two men connected the nozzle and the pumping started with a low thrum of the engine.

But from that same corner under the back steps, small pieces of furniture were created, fillets of golden wood peeling from Daddy's plane like slivers of hair, the grain smooth and ready to be chiselled, jointed, angled, attached by the nails held between his teeth, pounded by the hammer in his wiry hands.

Sometime during his riverside childhood he had learnt to saw and plane and join, chisel and nail. Only now can I re-imagine his apprentice craftsmanship, surrounded by mora and greenheart, red ants' nests, water snakes; imagine his father saying things like "Not like so Jim, like so." There were no technical colleges where boys learned these things; you learned from father to son, learned out of necessity.

In our back yard the coconut tree was king, taller than our house, full of water coconuts which an Indian boy skinned his knees to climb, cut, throw down into the yard, split open with one slice of his cutlass and offer us "sweet coconut water, nuh? Jelly? Allyuh wan some?" We would drink it straight, or chill it in the fridge; slide the soft white jelly down our throats. Ruby would grate it to make cook-up rice and sugar-cake. We all had a sweet tooth, and soon I learned to make fudge in the big black karhai, stirring slowly the mixture of milk and sugar, coconut or chocolate or vanilla, judging the right consistency, pouring it carefully into the square dish to cool, to set, to score into squares whilst begging sisters licked spoons, scraped the pan, dipped their fingers along the sides of the cooling pan.

\* \* \* \* \*

Like many of the people we knew, we grew up with servants. Ruby was the first one I remember, climbing up the back steps, chatting with Mummy in the kitchen, cooking and cleaning, washing and feeding clothes through the mangle so they came out flattened like the cutout dolls and clothes we got from magazines. Then for some reason, Ruby left, and in came a couple of odd women.

First the Jewel Thief, a girl from Stanleytown who stole all my mother's gold jewellery *and* Daddy's love letters. The loss of these love letters upset me no end when I learned about this, thinking how wonderful it would have been to have read them, and to learn something of Daddy as a Young Man. Even now the loss is stark, because on the whole I remember my father as a disciplinarian; he, like so many other Guyanese parents, was very strict, and quick to reach for the cane or his belt. These letters would have left a record of another side of him, a loving, gentler side I liked to imagine. Daddy must have thought he had died and gone to heaven, catching such a young sweet girl as my mother. But then again, my mother might never have let me read them, might have torn them up as she tends to do, during any of the many transitions in her life. She is not like me; doesn't harbour letters, locks of hair.

My father had apparently gone chasing after the Jewel Thief to her house in Stanleytown, but her man-friend had come to the door and said "She never steal nothing," and "Prove it," and had threatened to put his dog on Daddy, some half-starved mongrel foaming at the mouth. So that was that.

Then came a girl who was a Seventh Day Adventist, who boarded with us as she lived too far away, and who 'downed tools' after six as her religion decreed. After her, Mad Maria was employed, called 'mad' (of course not to her face) because she was a bit 'simple', 'not all there'; (language, of course, from non politically correct days). She was fair-skinned with African hair, couldn't cook, and cleaned in a manner described as 'top-top'. Whilst banging pots and pans around she would sing hymns and spirituals, and always had a hopeful grin. We would come home from school to hear her singing "What a friend we have in Jeesus" and

"Jeroosalem, Jeroosalem" at the top of her voice. A staunch Catholic (probably why she was employed in the first place) she made even my mother, herself a swift and constant runner to church, comment on her devotion. On Good Friday, Easter Sunday, and Christmas Eve, when all the sinners of the world crawled out from dark corners, she stood waiting an hour before the church door opened, then sprinted to the front pew and settled herself in prime position to swivel round as one by one and two by two New Amsterdam's Catholics filed in.

"She has to go," Daddy said. "What is the purpose of having a servant who can't cook?" Not that my mother couldn't cook; but she had enough to do with looking after us, coming home from school, stomachs rumbling, hungry for a lunch of stew beef or chowmein, a tea of butterflaps and biscuits, a supper of Vienna sausages or eggs or ham or cheese and bread, before Ovaltine, homework, bed. Ruby came back. I didn't know how long she'd been away or why; that wasn't children business. I distinctly remember her being there at the time of the fire, in 1965, but then she left again, and in came Baby.

Baby, whose real name was Norma, was part of our extended family, related to Doodoo and Wallace. Doodoo had been brought to Williamsburg in 1945, at the age of one month old, as was Wallace, to be brought up by Mother and Daddy J.

It was Baby whom I connect with being present through my teenage years, and who would su-su with Mummy in the kitchen as they sliced or washed or fried or used the mangle. Once to my utter shame and disgrace I actually heard them discussing *my period*! My period!

Baby and Doodoo's two brothers, Gordon and Godfrey, went to my school, Berbice High. Gordon was one of the school's best runners; he became Athletics Champion on more than one occasion. It was he who would come to stay with us nights at the time of Daddy's ghost, when it was said people knew there wasn't a man in the house anymore and would take advantage. When I think of the fate of our poor dog Rio I know there was some truth in that. But, you know, I can't see how a seventeen-year-old schoolboy could have been put in such a role as our protector, or how he could have deterred anyone set on doing us harm! Was he supposed to protect us from the dead or the living?

The relationship between Mummy and the women who worked for us appeared to flow easily, moving between the chatter of girlfriends and the position of employer and employed.

In any case it was different with Baby, as she was almost a relative and my mother herself was no stranger to country living or hard work; she'd fetched water, swept with pointer brooms, scrubbed steps and washboards with brushes and coal tar soap, fed chickens, and cleaned out fowl coops; worked the vegetable garden, shelled peas, picked weevils from the flour. Their life was a far gap from us 'town children'. They had been brought up using outside toilets and bathrooms placed way down the back yard with a corrugated or tin roof. This was never the favourite part of our visits to Williamsburg, and later Kwakwani, where we put off going to the toilet as long as we dared. Opening that creaking door, clocking the dark inside for spiders, *never* shutting the door completely, scared of sitting over the dark pit, using newspaper to wipe your bottom...

In St John Street, Mummy always had her hand turned to something, seeming to spend as much time in the kitchen as Baby did; in any case she would have been quite happy to run her own household. "But this is Town," she had been told from day one. "We not living in the country now, you know, Elizabeth."

It's hard to understand now some of our way of life then. Why, for instance, did we have chamber pots under our beds (which we used during the nights) when the toilet was just down the hall? Some Victorian throwback? Didn't we cotton on we had electric light? They had had potties up the country, which was understandable, but in New Amsterdam?

My mother in her new role of domestic employer obviously had qualms about certain things...she insisted we children emptied our potties before the servants came to work, that the servants were showed as much respect as any other adult, and Daddy insisted time and time again that we girls should pull our weight, and as we grew older we were delegated washing-up and cleaning duties in order that we didn't grow up lazy.

"These girls will not grow up lazy, servant or not," he said.

So Des and I had to take turns each week, alternating between 'house' and 'kitchen'. Kitchen meant getting up early and making Daddy's breakfast when his trips to Kwakwani were done and he landed a day job at Everton, became Commodore. Kitchen meant you had to wash the wares after dinner, clear the table and leave it tidy. Leave the pots in soak for Baby. Wait for Yonnette to finish eating. Yonnette pretended she was a baby for a long long time, way past the time she started school. And Mummy, holding on to her 'last row', still feeding her. Nobody was allowed to leave the table till everybody finish. Yonnette dawdled and dawdled. I got vexed when I was in the kitchen. It meant I had less time for reading.

Book and me were bosom friends. Book and me washed up together, Book propped up on the windowsill with the guava tree leaning over to see what he was saying. Wet hands didn't bother Book, Katy was so busy Doing, and The Hardy Boys were so busy solving mysteries, plus my hands were so slow washing up that my page-turning hand had time to dry. In any case Book knew that soon he and I would be in bed, under the sheets with the torchlight, gone nine o'clock.

House too had its good times and its bad times. Putting away the ironing, making up the beds, changing the sheets at the weekend were okay as okay goes. That polished floor was a different thing altogether. Before the floor shine you had to sweep it, before it shine you had to wash it, before it shine you had to get down on your knees and rub it and scrape it with the scraper, on your knees with your nice long fingernails. Sweeping was a long dusty affair. Guiding the dust from the gallery through the sitting room, not allowing any to fall through the cracks and annoy the people downstairs. Some of the floorboards had large cracks and your eye would get drawn there, hypnotise watching Downstairs go about their business in their singlet and slip. The polishing was slave labour. Dipping in the tin of Mansion Polish with the polishing cloth, applying and buffing, moving backwards on your knees like a pilgrim. Was that where the daydreaming started? Watching the mahogany wood darken and shine, the grain preen itself like one of the cats; the shapes that suggested themselves, the wings of swans, the tendrils of hair, the spires of castles jumping out of Book through my mind, stretching themselves like lizards underneath the polishing cloth. They'd travel later into the borders of my exercise books and rampage across my drawing book. No wonder my mother, having gone to market and returned, could never get over her amazement at how a little polishing could take up my whole Saturday morning.

But the worst, the very worst thing about House was the front steps. The back steps wasn't so bad because it was hidden from the road and you could fling that dust pellmell if nobody was looking. What does a little dust on a back step matter? Fling it to hell and go over the washing line and the septic tank. The dounze tree watched, gathering up her leaves like some old woman hoisting her crinoline. I was convinced some Dutch mistress ghost lived there, or some unfortunate slave woman. You heard all these stories about mistresses and dead babies, navel strings.

But the front steps, the front steps was Shame. Shame that people passing would see me with a broom or a bucket and pail in my hand. Double Shame if one of my friends should happen to pass by on their bicycle, or call in even, and see me with not only a pointer broom, but God forgive me, a *mop*. And Mummy couldn't understand either how I could do that whole front steps in less than five minutes flat.

Both Ruby and Baby, in their respective times, would eat their lunch in the kitchen; however, after school we'd come up the front steps to find them sitting at the dining table with Mummy, drinking Red Rose tea and eating Marie biscuits. The question, why didn't they sit at the dining table all the time? was never answered; like many other questions, the response was "It's not for children to know everything," or "You think you're a Big Woman, cross-questioning me?" You could quicktime get a slap for opening your mouth.

Never mind about the swing Daddy had made, or the see-saw, neither of which any other children in the street possessed; we liked nothing better than to play next door, or in the street. Hopscotch on the concrete in next door's yard; skipping with groups of neighbour children with thick ship's rope stretched across the road, to rhymes composed about love, marriage and babies, jumbies and sailors; hula hoop competitions of belly and hip-bone motion keeping the hoop circling whilst hands clapped; and the simple game of jacks, which we played squatting on the bridge. Was a thing to get a new packet of jacks, gleaming silver through the plastic, the old ones long lost, rolled under the bridge into the gutter, replaced by pebbles. Was a thing to toss that ball in the air, grab the jacks before it fell, a thing of skill, practice, determination.

Loretta and Aloyius lived in one of four houses in the yard opposite, owned by an old Portuguese man whose name I can't remember. Their mother, 'Aunty Lel', had had an accident with a kerosene stove when she was young, and half of her face was burnt and scarred. But she went about her business as if nothing had ever happened, day in day out carrying on with her cooking and cleaning and children and market. In the afternoons she would relax in her gallery, face to the window. She and my mother would have cross words sometimes, usually to do with us children fighting over something or other. Tempers ran hot in the tropics; it was not unusual for fights to break out amongst women over some trifle. Thankfully this wasn't my mother's style, though she would defend her children to the death, and wasn't afraid to confront anyone who wronged us. But overall the policy of good manners and respectful distance maintained domestic peace.

Lel's children's father had another family up the Corentyne. I wouldn't know if there was any order in his visits to St John Street; we would just hear the motorbike and the cut of the engine before he wheeled it in the yard. They didn't have servants, and Loretta was much more knowledgeable about many things than me and my sisters, and knew more about cooking than all of us put together. We didn't have a clue when it came to a bush cook for instance, which we did in the yard; only Loretta knew how to start a fire and keep it in, would get real rice and real herbs, reach for greens growing on the vine and know what it was, whilst we still pretended, with mud pies and dolly plates.

Daddy could never understand why, with the see-saw and the swing sitting there, any of his daughters should want to go anywhere but their own yard. But we did, even though you always had to ask, beg, beseech, promise no we wouldn't go in nobody house, no we wouldn't touch nobody things, no we wouldn't open our mouth and spread nobody business, yes we would say please and thank you, no we mustn't go and eat up people food, yes if we had a drink we wouldn't drain the glass.

There were all sorts of rules which we were meant to live by. Although outwardly it was a social, drop-in anytime society, it was nevertheless a society that acknowledged the individual right to privacy. There were just some things you did not do. As children it was always being drummed into us that there was a difference between adults and us. Adults were always right and children "didn't know they were born yet". The word 'but' was *not* allowed. You never interrupted. You dare not eyeball an adult. You dare not put your hand on your hips and pretend you were a 'big' (adult) woman. Never say the word 'drunk'. Never refer to a man's pants (trousers). 'Expecting' was better than 'pregnant'. Licks was the rule of the day.

You could go play next door yes, but agreement had to be made between the adults. You never went anywhere near an adult's room, or touched anything that did not belong to you. You never went visiting at mealtimes, never invited yourself anywhere, always addressed adults by their title or as Aunt or Uncle, and never, never passed adults in the street (whether you knew them or not) without raising your head and saying a good morning or good afternoon.

*Manners maketh man.* It came back to haunt you if you did forget. *I saw that Margaret, Captain Harris daughter, and she pass me straight-straight, wearing she miniskirt. Gon end up bad that one.*

Everybody got licks.

Guyanese parents didn't believe in sparing the rod and spoiling the child. The boy over the back hollered as his mother chased him round the yard with a pointer broom.

"Lord Mummy, don't beat me no more! I ain gon do it anymore!"

"You damn right you won't! You tek your eyes and pass me?" We'd hear the cane thwack against his legs whilst we giggled from the backsteps. Then it would be our turn. Mummy would chase me round the dining table with a hairbrush.

"Come here you little devil! I'm going to give you what for!" She'd try to grab my arm as I scrambled under the table, the brush rising in the air, then landing on my bottom. I would open my mouth wide and scream, wanting everyone to hear my suffering and the injustice.

"It's not me! I didn't do it."

"Don't argue with me! Is only you father you listen to? He gon cut you tail for true!"

On one of the rare occasions Desiree got licks, it had to do with Aunty. Mummy was making a cake and we were helping stir until our arms got tired and we escaped downstairs to Mummy's warning, "Don't go telling Aunty I making cake!"

We wandered over to Aunty's yard, where we'd recently buried a rat. We'd found it under the backsteps, picked it up by its tail and placed it in an old mincer, and proceeded to prepare for a bush cook, gathering what we thought were herbs. But the sight of the tail hanging over the side made us feel sorry for it; he could have children and a wife! The thought stilled our hands and we decided to give it a decent burial instead, in a cardboard coffin with a crucifix made from a palm leaf, like Palm Sunday, a wreath of daisy chains, and prayers, in Latin of course, *Spiritus Sanctus*, and a sprinkle of incense from an old watering can.

So we wander to find the grave but can't find it for looking; all we can see in the dirt are footprints from Aunty's rubber slippers and Cousin Lucille's tyre tracks. Aunty's hanging her washing out and asks what we're doing and of course we can't tell and that's when Desiree bursts out about Mummy making a cake.

"Is who birthday?" Aunty asks, and I glare at Des, head back to our yard, climb our front steps and tell.

Elizabeth's relationship with her sister-in-law fuels the

slaps that Desiree gets, and Des is the biggest cry-baby, grey eyes wide with indignation, that this mother who is her universe should dare to chastise her.

"I told you not to tell her!"

Elizabeth at twenty five is not out dancing or driving a car, is not raising a daiquiri to her red lips by a blue pool, but has three children to raise, a husband who is old enough to be her father, a church which she loves but which does not love her, interfering relatives and step-parents who treat her as a child.

"You can't do anything in this place without everybody knowing your business!"

Aunty, following the sound of the commotion, came pelting up our front steps, exclaiming: "Elizabeth! I know why you're beating that child! You think I want your stupid cake?"

And then there's the time when I rise from the dining table sullen and slow, like Marilyn Monroe, or so I think. My hips are willing themselves to curve beneath my cotton housedress, to cradle and extend limbs I hope will shimmer when I stroll along Main Street, legs which by some miracle would have filled out from these skeletal knees and ankles. The backs of my fingers brush carelessly over my hipbones as I head for the gallery windows.

"Young lady!"

Daddy's voice stops me in my tracks.

What did I do? Forget to ask leave? Take my plate in?

I turn.

There's something about the tone of his voice. He's still sitting at the dining table, knife and fork in hand.

"Yes Daddy?"

"Who the hell you think you are waltzing off the table like that without an *Excuse Me*? And the walks! You think you are a big woman?"

He threw the knife down on the table.

"Get into the bedroom!"

"No Daddy! I didn't do nothing Daddy!"

"Don't you dare answer me back! God dammit! Mary, fetch me the cane."

Elizabeth tried to intervene.

"Jim, she didn't mean anything by it. Margaret like to show off."

"She not going to show off in this house! She not going to wine her tail like some Pitt Street woman!"

He grabbed me by the arm and marched me into their bedroom and threw me face down on the bed. I began to cry before the first lash. The cane whistled through the air, landing two, three times through my thin cotton dress. I was confused. What had I done?

"No daughter of mine is going to grow up acting like a tramp!"

"That's enough, Jim!" I sense my mother grab the cane from him. He was blowing like a bull in a ring.

She sat next to me, lifting me up from the bed.

"Come child, stop crying. You mustn't rile you father so."

The next time I walk I remember.


We're playing in the yard.

"Sticks and stones may break my bones but words will never hurt."

"That not true. Somebody say something nasty, that worse."

"Licks does bun and cool."

"Mummy licks like mosquito bites."

"Daddy beat bad, man."

"Sister lash me and Coreen yesterday cos we din go back to school after lunch."

"Mr. Beharry give me four whups las week because I din do my stupid Latin."

"Royston mother beat he so bad he holler Jesus Mary and Joseph!"

"That's because she black. Black people does beat badder than anybody."

"You mustn't say 'Black', you must say 'Negro'."

"That not true, Coolie people worse."

"You mustn't say 'Coolie', you must say 'Indian'."

"And look what Tita do to Lucille, make she kneel on the cheese grater for ten whole minutes."

"That nothing, that woman in Georgetown put her chile finger under she sewing machine needle."

"Radio say this morning a thief man get thirty lashes."

"When I grow up I not gon beat my chile."

"You mad? How else you gon get them to behave?"

Our next door neighbour owned a Corentyne bus, *The Lady Lindy*, which amazingly could be driven down our narrow street, and amazingly be parked in their yard, and it was always entertaining to watch it being negotiated backwards without it getting wedged in the gutter. My bedroom window looked directly into their gallery and on the rare occasions when I visited I would stand and look across at my window, half expecting to see myself standing there.

I liked going up their closed-in stairs, trellised all the way up, and into their living room. I went through a spell of being mesmerised by the brother's Lego, which had been sent from abroad. There was something about the tiny bricks and minuscule windows and their facility of being able to receive sections of themselves and be transformed into rooms and buildings, offices and schools, that held my interest for indeterminate lengths of time. I'd get lost in a Lego world just as I would when racing toy cars in the borders of the linoleum in the dining room...*what you bothering with cars for, you not a boy!*...or scooting up the dounze and guava trees or attempting to skin up the coconut trunk the way the Indian boy did.

Inevitably the mother would clear her throat or someone would be sent to fetch me; Desiree's small voice would follow her rap on the door, trickling up the closed-in stairs, "G'afternoon Mrs...Mummy say Margaret have to come home now," and I would drag myself home unwillingly, angry at being taken out of a world, angry at Daddy not being able to afford a Lego set for me, angry at Des for being the messenger.

Des loved reading, just like me, and there were no more peaceful moments than the ones where we were both curled up with The Hardy Boys or a Famous Five Adventure. She was still Mummy's girl though, and somehow I was charged with being Daddy's. *You never answer your Daddy back, just take your eyes an pass me!*

We would be forever borrowing books; from next door, from downstairs, from Loretta, from Lorna, from Cora, from Christopher across the yard: comics, westerns, story books, any and everything. Many arguments ensued over books, whose it was, who borrowed it from who and didn't give it back, who crease over the page so, who had the cheek to lend it to their friend without asking. I doubt whether books would have had the impact they did if we had had TV. The outside world impacted on us through these books, and it was always a shock to raise your head and find you were sitting on the gallery chair in a steamy room with long windows and not on a snow-covered mountain in the Alps.

We would never know who would be sitting in the kitchen chair when we came home from school. It could be a wandering beggar, or someone's 'poor relation' family, it could be Cookie. Cookie and I didn't see eye to eye.

My mother would always tell me off when she saw my face change as I spotted Cookie in the chair.

"Say Good Afternoon to Cookie!"

And Cookie would squelch out of her mash-mouth, "Don't bother wid the chile Mrs Harris, de time will come."

Cookie was called Cookie because she used to cook for Daddy's family before he got married to Mummy. She was old-old; dry skin, pink-gummed mash-mouth, yellow eyes, grey dry-grass hair. Sometimes, if a babysitter was in short supply, Cookie was roped in. I knew that complaints would be flying. *Margaret this and Margaret that. Not like Desiree and Mary those good children, but that one...*

When Baby Yonnette came along, we watched in disgust as Cookie mashed up her bread in milk and fed it to her on a spoon. She didn't know the delicacy of the operation of soaking bread, how you just had to dip it in your tea-tea or chocolate or Ovaltine, carry it to your mouth before the peanut butter drips, before the bread dropped into the cup.

Poor Yonnette, born in 1961, was just a baby and ate it uncomplainingly, sucking it willingly off the spoon like an open-beaked baby bird while Cookie sang some stupid lullaby, "Sweet little dumpling, Daddy gone a-hunting."

Cookie did not like me one bit. She called me Hardears, and if any of the children cried, screeched "Margritttttt! What you doin to you sistuh!?" Like the time of the Destruction of The Tent. A master tent. I remember it clear-clear. Mummy had gone out somewhere, matinée most likely, and Cookie was babysitting. We had spent the best part of an afternoon out on the front porch, draping an arrangement of tablecloths and towels acquired from the linen chest across the veranda rail and the banisters, pegged by an assortment of clothes pegs and diaper pins. Cookie must have been snoozing indoors, and on waking to the unaccustomed quietness, was immediately alert. *When children too quiet them up to sumting.* She shuffled to investigate as was her duty, and came upon a shameless display of Mrs Harris's best things out in the open for All The World to see.

Underneath, in the twilight cave, we had the dolls all lined up for their cod liver oil when all of a sudden, like in the story of the three little pigs, the roof of our 'house' was lifted right over the top of our heads. And there was Cookie the wolf, all wrinkled skin and pink gums "Eh eh! Look at mih crosses! Margrit you not shame!? You Mummy good-good things! Is tiefman you trying to attract? You is the oldest, you should set example! Break up this dam fool thing you hear! Or is two slap you gon get as The Lord is my witness!"

But when Cookie sang, I sat at the edge of her circle. It was a thing and a half to hear Cookie sing:

*Pretty little butterfly*
*What you do all day?*
*Flitting in the garden, nothing do but play*
*Nothing do but play mih darling*
*Nothing do but play*
*Fly butterfly, fly butterfly, take yourself away*

Church, church, church. Each time we passed the Roman Church, we had to make the sign of the cross. And every Saturday, every Sunday, there was Confession, Mass, Sunday School, Catechism, First Communion Class, Confirmation Class, Choir Practice, CCD.

*Bless me father for I have sinned, it has been xxx days since my last confession. I pinched my sister and wouldn't share my book, I thought Cookie was a dry up ole higue even though I know Jesus Sees All.*

One Our Father and six Hail Marys.

Bells ringing. The faithful running. The choir in the balcony hurling hymns above and below. The organ pumping. Mad Maria in her seat long time. High heel shoes clip up Church of Ascension steps, pause at the Holy Communion font; make the sign of the Cross, clip-clop up aisle. Soft shoe shuffle in the pews. Church hats, prayer books, gloves, smooth and trim. The Ralph girls in chiffon, satin edging. New Amsterdam in bonnets and bows, white feather bandeaus, suits and ties, crisp cotton, organdie and can-cans, serge and satin, white socks, whitened shoes, polished shoeshine shoes.

Bodies hot and squeezing, arms and elbows touching. Talcum powder, eau de cologne, Lifebuoy soap, Old Spice. Scratch of lace, a hum like bees, bottoms and knees genuflecting, shuffling, adjusting waistbands, cufflinks, gloves; thumbing missals and rosaries, bangles and earrings jangling. Coughs, sneezes, white handkerchiefs blowing. Children, shoe heels scraping, noses itching, faces enticed to the left, to the right, to the back, ears and noses twisted round by adults to face the front. Altar boys and incense, copper pendulums, Father gliding from aisle to pulpit to Communion rail. Stained glass windows, Kyrie Eleisons, altar boys like winged angels.

Aunt Marie gets the benefit of Mad Maria's stare as she enters the church by the side door as Father and his altar boys are proceeding up the aisle. Then up we rise, stand up, sit down, kneel down, pray. Open hymn books, croak and croon, in tune, out of tune, Body and Blood. *Holy Mother of God, Pray for us...Pray for us...Pray for us.* Father, head back, swigs the wine. Those for the Eucharist stand in line.

All except Mummy. All except Mummy. She kneels in the pew, head bowed, threading the beads of her rosary. My mother is not allowed to take the Holy Sacrament because. Because she married my Daddy in the Anglican Church.

Why did she marry my Daddy in the Anglican Church? You could not get a better Catholic than my mother. Not a mass does she miss, not a prayer does she not know, a refrain she cannot answer, even in Latin. "Kyrie Eleison," her lips whisper, "Christe Eleison." She rises at four in the morning for Benediction, hosts rosary sessions in her house during the month of May.

In the quiet our eyes wander from missals to new feather hats, to fat bottoms wedged in the pew, to the secret door at the right of the altar that leads to the convent through which the nuns glide, and only on special days, First Communion Days, Confirmation Days, do the children follow ushered by godmothers who bear down on you with face powder cheeks, bearing gifts of new rosaries and small white Bibles, silver medals, and new names.

We'd all had to be re-born, myself, Des and Mary, re-christened, re-named, washed clean of being Anglican, Daddy's church, where our parents had been married and where we'd first been christened because, because, because. At first they'd made a pact; Daddy had two of us accompanying him to his church, and Mummy took the other two to the Roman Church but somehow now, Mummy has us all safely in Rome whilst Daddy walks alone. But little Elo still stands half-in, half-out of the Catholic Church, whilst Father and the Sisters say *Bless you my child*. Half-in, half-out too of the whist drives, the bridge afternoons. The English *ladies* by birth or design with cars and shop-bought clothes, and vacations *back home*. My godmother is Mrs Ferdinand (yes, the wife of the same Dr Ferdinand, who'd lifted me feet first and silent into the world, slapped me into making my very first sound). Now Margaret Anita becomes Mary Theresa, *Theresa*, of Lisieux, not that other one, the Spanish one, from Ávila. Margaret Anita Mary *Theresa*.

And on Feast days, dressed in our very best frocks and polished shoes we file out of the church and form a procession, circle the church via Pope Street, carrying candles and singing. During May month we sing *Sweet Sacrament Divine* and escort the statue of Our Lady on a cart, garlanded with flowers; and there might be a stand-in Mary, one of the Portuguese girls, of course, her long brown hair cascading beneath the mantle of blue. At Christmas too, the chosen one would sit on the cart cradling a white baby doll.

I couldn't imagine it then, but can now...other processions, centuries old, turning out onto mountain passes and Roman roads, the hills of Funchal. The singing and the incense, the suitable clothes, the flowers, the statues. Maybe a little less traffic.

Daddy, what do you think when you stroll to church on your own? Sharp in your light grey suit, white shirt, striped tie, angled Panama hat? Pass all those families dressed to kill all along Main Street. Sometimes your sister Ena is with you, cutting a fine figure herself as she must, for scissors, cloth and thread are her daily bread. No less than a dozen people will tip their hats to you, at least a score of "Good Mornings" between St John and Trinity Streets, whilst all the church bells of New Amsterdam are pealing their iron souls out, clanging their authenticity on the true path to Heaven. In and out of church, good, affable, sensible, well-meaning Protestants, excited by life, cushioned by history, freed from all that Roman nonsense. What kind of a husband are you? Couldn't you make your wife walk alongside you? I guess it's the old case of leading the horse to water but...Does your heart lift nevertheless? Do you step from the church door re-energised, fulfilled, regardless of the fact that no young legs had scuffed their shoes against yours in that English pew, no-one had paused to ruffle your daughters' heads, admire your fresh young wife? And you walk along Main Street, join us outside our church door where the anointed tumble out into the sunshine like a scatter of butterflies, bodies as light as their newly blessed souls.

# 9

# Rum and Coca-Cola

Uncle Henry is pounding the coffee table with his fists; they're huge and red with blond hairs sprouting from the knuckles and white lines in the flesh where the sun doesn't catch. He's singing *She'll be coming round the mountain* at the top of his voice and every time he gets to the *yi yi yippie yi* bit, my Daddy and the sailors join in, loud and raucous, and merry.

Baby brings in another bottle of XM Rum and picks up the empty ice bucket.

Daddy's guitar was already in business across his lap and Uncle Henry had pulled my mother out of the kitchen and had waltzed her through the dining room.

Uncle Henry wasn't really our uncle. He was one of the American bosses at the bauxite plant at Everton. With two shots of rum he became redder and loosened his shirt collar, called Daddy 'Jimbo' and slapped everybody's back. Rum made everybody friends, but even though the sailors and Mr Hartman were relaxing on the leatherette settee they still called Jimbo 'Captain'. *Even* after he became Commodore.

We'd been hiding behind the dining room partition giggling. Was a time to be treasured when Daddy got merry, true-true. That strict-faced Daddy disappeared. This one laughed, and played his guitar. This was a time fuh true.

Uncle Henry kept beckoning us.

"Come, children, come! Come sing this lil song with me...*She'll be wearing six white horses when she comes*...hey, that's not right, is it?"

We giggled behind our hands.

"*She'll be riding six white h...* Jimbo, how come such an ugly chap like you can have such beautiful daughters? Why so shy, sweetheart?"

My mother huffs.

"This one shy? She's got a plaster for every sore!"

Uncle Henry laughs.

"Naa…ahh. Look at those baby blues. Innocence, oh innocence. I tell you Jimbo, this one's a heartbreaker!"

One of the sailors piped up.

"C'pn is true you know, how come a fella like you got all these lovely daughters?"

"They take after their mother, man! You have to ask? Liz, come take a drink nuh!"

My mother screws up her face at the rum. "You want to get me tipsy?"

We've seen Mummy *tipsy*. Once her giggling turned to tears and her legs were kicking as Daddy picked her up and took her into the bedroom.

"Come man, take a sip, this is nectar man, nectar. You know all that time explorers looking for El Dorado? Well it right here, man! Liquid gold. Solid one hundred per cent Guyana gold."

"…*She'll be coming round…*What's this one's name, Jimbo?"

"Which one? This lickle one? This little brown-skin brown-eyed girl of mine? Mary man, sweet Mary. I tell you Henry, when the Lord was giving out graces this one took all. Mary by name and Mary by nature. Come Mary, sit on Daddy lap."

My sister inched herself shyly to where he's sitting in his favourite place, the rocking chair by the radio. The conch shell uncurls his ears. Mary's brown eyes look up at Daddy, weighing him up, then he puts his guitar down and pulls her up. She nestles back against him, burrowing into the cigarettes and Old Spice scent, legs stretched out along his. Her little plaits stick out like antennae. Daddy hums *There's a brown girl in the ring…*and the others join in, *Fa la la la la, a brown girl in the ring…*

Mary giggles and hides her face against his shirt.

…*Sweet lika sugar in a plum! Bum! Bum!*

Fists on the table. Laughter.

"This little girl open the gate for me every morning you know boys! Step and step with me going downstairs, wait till I drive out. And who you think waiting, swinging on the gate when I come home, watching out for she daddy?"

"You's a lucky man, C'pn."

"You think I don't know that? Man, you can't tell me what I know already! But Henry, you glass empty man! Where you think you are, America? Liz, fill up the man glass nuh, you want give Guyanese hospitality a bad name?"

One of the sailors picks up the guitar, starts strumming with less grace than my father.

*Brown skin girl stay home and mind baby*
*Brown skin girl stay home and mind baby*
*I going away in a sailing boat and if I don't come back*
*Throw 'way the damn baby!*

Mummy has taken a sip of rum but passes it to Uncle Compton, visiting with another uncle from Georgetown. He was another one always telling me what to do. Though there was that time he and Aunty had words and he saved me:

"Why you beating that child?"

"Is my brother's chile, I have every right to beat her"

"Well, is my sister's child so gimme the damn cane!"

The last time he visited he'd got *merry* and had fallen asleep in Yonnette's cot, his legs dangling over the side! *Disgusting!* I can't remember where my poor baby sister ended up sleeping. He even had the cheek to take my kitten Mitsy, *my* kitten! out of my arms telling me I wasn't stroking her right!

"Y'all just give me a beer," Mummy says. "Is this party going on all day?"

"All work and no play makes Jack a dull boy!"

"All play and no work makes June pretty lively!"

This comes from Uncle Henry, who hiccups as he says it, and the sailors giggle and snort into their glasses.

My parents exchange glances.

Uncle Henry wipes his beard with the back of his hand. He's giggling like a schoolboy, stealing small glances at my father from beneath his big eyebrows.

"How's Esther, Henry?" my mother asks, head back and eyebrows arched.

My father cast her a look.

"Esther? Oh Esther! Let's not talk about Esther, Liz!"

Daddy takes the guitar away from the sailor who'd been plucking tuneless chords. Mary is still sitting on his lap, wriggling to accommodate the guitar, and he starts to play something by Jose Feliciano. Her fingers tap the side of the guitar.

Desiree had moved out onto the porch where Yonnette was humming the Feliciano tune as she settled the kittens into the doll's pram. Little mews could be heard in-between the picking of the strings, and dulled voices from the street below.

"Liz, you know honey..." Uncle Henry's American accent cuts over the music. "This life does not suit everyone, y'know what I mean? It's real hard to leave your country and settle into a new way of life, you get me?"

One of the sailors winks at me; he's humming under his breath *Pretty blue eyes please come out to play so I can tell you what I have to say...*

Baby comes in from the kitchen. She has her going-home dress on.

"Excuse me Mrs..."

"Oh Baby, you finish up?"

"Yes Mrs Harris, you want me to do anything more?"

"No thanks girl, you go on. I'll clear up after this lot."

"Good afternoon Captain, good afternoon everybody."

"Walk good Baby."

"Mind the road, sweet girl!"

One of the sailors gives her a wink. She cuts her eye on him, flounces her skirt, and heads for the back door.

Uncle Henry is staring into his glass. My mother beckons me over.

"Girl, go and fetch some ice from the freezer."

It's cool in the kitchen. The lunch things are all washed and put away; the wooden worktops and vinyl floor shine. The mop is still dripping on the back porch and the smell of ripe guavas hangs heavy through the kitchen window. The smell of pepperpot draws me, simmering away from the black pot on the stove. I lift the lid without thinking and drop it straight away. The lid clatters onto the floor and rich drops of black stew speckle the linoleum.

A shout from the living-room:

"Margaret! Is what you doing? I send you to fetch ice not break up the place!"

"Is nothing. I coming in a minute."

I run my fingers quickly under the tap then grab the mop from outside.

"What you doing, girl?"

I jump. The Georgetown uncle.

"Nuttin," I mutter.

"That don't look like nothing to me. Why you can't do as you're told, eh?"

"It was a accident. I burn my hand."

"Well is God punish you. I don't know what you children doing hanging round big people business anyway. Why y'all don't go outside and play?" He pulls the mop from me and waves me away. "Look g'wan, g'wan. I gon get the blasted ice. Y'all blasted mother spoil you is what."

I slid back through the dining room. Could I get through to my bedroom without anybody seeing me? Out on the front porch Yonnette was trying to force her old baby bonnet on the cat's head but she'd wriggled away and stood glowering on the top step, keeping a watchful eye on her kittens.

"My wife worked in Michigan you know, this kind of life is new to her, and she can't stand the heat."

"You have to give these things time Henry."

"Margaret, what you standing there doolally for and what happen to the ice?"

"Uncle say..."

"She useless man, useless. Here."

Uncle sweeps aside the ashtrays and glasses and makes room for the ice bucket.

"Ah, don't give the man a hard time Liz, you know how things are in this country."

Mummy's eyes swing from me to Uncle Henry.

"Well it makes things a little difficult for me, Henry. You know I have to be nice to both of them."

"Mary jump down, there's a good girl, go and play with your sisters."

Mary stands there looking lost.

"Yes, yes, y'all run off and play," Uncle Compton says. "Elo, you really shouldn't have these children listening to big people story."

Mummy gives her half-brother a slanting, piercing look from her brown eyes.

"*Don't* call me Elo! *I* have these children listening? *I* have them listening?"

"Well Elo, you and me know how children must be seen and not heard!"

"Y'all stop squabbling, children!" Daddy intervened. "Man, this is all the ice?"

"Eh heh, the rest ain set yet."

"Margaret, go to Girdharry shop and ask for a block of ice. Here's fifty cents."

"Yes Daddy."

"And wait," he grabbed my hand, "who's Daddy's girl then?"

"I thought was Mary," I muttered.

"You thought...!"

He threw his head back and laughed. "You's a jealous girl, eh? But Mary don't give me no backchat, y'know."

"I ain backchatting you, Daddy." *As if I would!* "Hmmm." He reached out and pulled my ponytail. "You'll always be my firstborn though." He pulled out some more change from his pocket.

"Here, buy some chocolate or sweetie for y'all."

"Thanks Daddy!"

"Hey Margaret!" Uncle Henry was reaching in his pocket too. "How much did that miser give you?"

I opened my palm.

"Twenty-five cents! O man! The last of the big spenders, eh Jimbo?" He stood up, ungainly, large red knees in khaki shorts, perspiration damp on his thighs. He rustled in his pocket.

"Here's a dollar sweetheart, treat you and your sisters."

I could sense my sisters' antennae growing, curling round the doorway. Even Yonnette piped up, "Sweeties!"

One whole dollar and twenty-five cents! A whole bar of chocolate was treat enough, or a tube of Smarties, which Mummy usually brought back from the pictures for us to share. We were rich, man! Rich-rich. Won't even have to share!

"Wait, wait!" One of the sailors raised up his hands. "Don't let C'pn say his first mate can't treat his children!"

Another twenty-five cents was dropped in my hand.

"Or his Chief Engineer!" Mr Hartman added, slapping more coins down on the table.

"Say thanks then, girl." Uncle glowered.

"Thanks Mr Hartman, thanks Uncle Henry, thanks Mr…"

"Phillips, darling."

I left when the going was good, but three pairs of hands were waiting for me on the porch.

"I coming with you, give me mine!"

"Daddy said me!"

"We can still come."

"No, I have to get ice too."

"Well you can't carry all yourself, plus you don't know what we want."

"Let's just you and me go."

"All right."

"Why I can't come too? Y'all always leave me out… Mummeeee!"

Mummy steamed out.

"What the hell is all this commotion? Margaret, you can't do a simple thing without carrying on?"

"Is not me! All o' them want fuh come!"

"Want *to* come. Well you can't. All four of you will get knock down on the road. Yonnette…you and Mary stay here. Desiree, you go with Margaret, and don't dawdle."

We galloped down the front steps to the ascent of Mary's wailing and Yonnette's high wild shriek. All of a sudden something hard hit me on the back of my knee. Desiree jumped away just in time to see the dolly pram bumping down the steps, kittens flying into the air.

"Oh my God! Jim!"

"Betsy!"

"Mitsy!"

"Blackie!"

"Cooks!"

Mummy's hands were chicken wings flapping, slapping Yonnette and Mary in turn. "Y'all bad-bad children! Why y'all do that?" Their caterwauling rose into the air. Mary was saying she never kick no pram, Yonnette that it was a 'naccident', and at the bottom of the steps kittens crawled out shaking their heads, adorned with purple bougainvillea.

Desiree and I cradled them up and kissed them, brushed them off, set them down on the concrete to see if they could walk. Their mother appeared, licking them and disappearing with them one by one under the bottom house.

"Are they all right?" Mummy called from upstairs. "You see what commotion could cause? They coulda broken their little necks! Y'all hise your tails and get the ice before I take your pocket piece away and put it in Father collection on Sunday!"

We flew out the yard.

"Girdharry or Daniel?"

"Daniel."

Girdharry's shop was only at the top of the road; Daniel's was across Main Street and had more choice...toy racing cars with picture postcards, cigarette sweets with photographs of movie stars like Elvis and Tab Hunter and Ava Gardner.

But Daniel sold wild canes too, and many a time one or the other of us had been sent to buy one because ours had mysteriously disappeared.

The worst thing was coming back down the street with a cane in your hand and the children in the street seeing you. *Nah nah nah nah nah somebody gon get get licks!* But this was treating time, not beating time; kicks time, not licks time. We crossed Main Street by the church, remembering to make the sign of the Cross. Mr Daniel raised his head as we walked in chorusing our *Good Afternoons*.

"Y'all mother and father all right?"

"Yes thank you, Mr Daniel."

"What y'all want?"

"A block of ice please Mr Daniel, four slabs of Cadbury chocolate..."

"Two packs of cigarette sweets..."

"Two ounce Love Heart sweeties..."

"A tube of Smarties..."

"And a bottle of Coca-Cola."

"...Please."

"Y'all come into a inheritance?"

We giggled.

"Entertaining then. We ain got no ice."

"We'll just have the sweeties then."

"And the coke. And the chocolate. Please."

We stopped by the church gate to light the cigarette sweetie, taking a long draw and sharing it, just like in the films. There was a picture card of Suzanne Pleshette looking *sexy*. Mrs G came flying out of the church and gave us a look.

"Y'all children loitering? G'wan home!"

We extinguished the cigarette slowly, tapping it carefully on the back of the pack before slipping it back in for later. Mr Girdharry was straightening the sacks of sugar. We tried to hide the feast behind our backs.

"Good afternoon, Mr Girdharry."

"Afternoon, children. Y'all hiding something?"

"No, Mr Girdharry."

"I does sell sweetie too, you know. Look." He points at the glass jars lined up on the counter.

"Can we have a block of ice please, Mr Girdharry?"

"Why? Mr Daniel ain got none?" He sucked his teeth then went out in the back where we could hear him hacking away. He came out with the ice wrapped in brown paper.

"Thank you Mr Girdharry."

"Hmmp," he said, turning back to his sugar sacks. Back down the street slowly, Desiree holding the ice close to her chest. We opened one of the chocolate bars and melt pieces in our palms, swirling it round, licking it off with small sweeps of our fingers.

"You know that June they was talking about?"

"Uncle Henry's fancy girl?"

"Mummy didn't take we to she apartment before market last week?'

"Eh heh, behind Penguin Hotel."

"I like she, she was nice."

"But Uncle Henry got a wife."

"So? Loretta Daddy got a wife."

"You think Daddy ever had a fancy girl?"

"Of course not! How you can even think of such a thing!"

"I don't know."

"Mummy must like she or we won't go there."

"More I think June like Mummy. She smiling all the time and getting out she fancy glasses."

"I think she showing off. Aunty say coolie like to show off, especially the country-come-to-town type."

"We better hurry, the ice melting."

Christopher was sitting on his bike by our front gate. He looked up at us from under a shiny flap of black hair.

"Y'all having a fête?"

"Mind you own business! I aksing you your business?"

"You finish with that cowboy book I lend you?"

"What cowboy book? You think I does read that rubbish?"

"You take it away before I finish it!"

"Well more fool you to let a girl take your book away. I'll look amongst my vast collection and see if I spy it."

"You're horrid to him," Desiree says as we go in the yard.

"Boys are stupid."

Daddy was passing pieces of paper round the room, one with a hole in it.

"Write down in that hole what the wife said to her husband on her wedding night."

Uncle looking disapproving. Uncle Henry had got even redder. Mummy had her eyebrows raised again.

The first mate says, "But C'pn I haven't got a wife."

"You ain got imagination?"

He scratched his head.

"I don't get it C'pn..."

"It simple man! Take the pencil, write *through* the hole on the paper underneath, what the wife said to her husband, or what you can *imagine* she said to her husband on their wedding night!"

"C'pn he can't imagine that at all! No woman foolish enough to try him!"

Mummy notices me lingering by the front door.

"Girl, go and put the ice in the freezer."

Their laughter followed me through to the kitchen where I chip some ice off for me and my sisters, drop it in a plastic cup. Through the kitchen window I could see Desiree sharing out the booty in the yard downstairs. I'd better hightail it down there myself or the feast will soon be gobbled up. But the continuing laughter from the living room was like a magnet. Why couldn't my parents be so light-hearted all the time? I glanced at the kitchen clock; Mummy hadn't even remembered Confession! I dawdled by the cooler. A determined fly was trying to squeeze himself through a crack in the mesh. Uncle Henry was saying something about Esther telling him all night that she was a good girl and that didn't warrant writing down. Mummy was getting giggly and said she needed a whole page. The first mate, who'd been staring confusedly at the pieces of paper, was saying, "But C'pn, even if I could imagine it, this hole too small."

At which point everybody in the room exploded into laughter and Daddy, once he'd got his voice back, spluttered out, "That's it man! That's just what the wife said on the wedding night!"

I had no idea what they were laughing at. In fact, all of a sudden they didn't look like grown-ups at all, but like that drawing in *Alice in Wonderland* of the Mad Hatter's Tea Party, laughing and spluttering into their glasses. I left them to it; escaping down the back steps with the cups of ice, joining my sisters by the swing where we drew on cigarette sweets and knocked plastic cups together chorusing, "Cheers!"

# 10

# Corentyne Tales: 1

We're driving up the Corentyne in Daddy's new pick-up truck. I'm six years old. Daddy turns off the road and bumps over a cattle grid and along a farm track. It smells different here, of grass and smoke and cow dung. It's flat country, grazing country, meadows and cattle, a creek, tufts of palms in the distance where the Corentyne River runs. We roll over another grid, into a yard just barely fenced in by wire mesh.

From the veranda Uncle Beau uncurls his long self, his blue eyes bright and laughing.

"Well, well! And who is this? Who is this! Carmelita! Come and see who the breeze blow in!"

He looks just like a cowboy, Uncle Beau does; with his cowboy hat and leathery skin, and eyes crinkled up at the corners. He lifts us up, one after the other squealing like piglets, legs wriggling from under our seersucker dresses. Aunty Carmelita, her round face shining, greets us with the Peepso game, teasing us out from behind Mummy's skirts. I loved this game since I was a baby; when Aunty Carmelita visited she would call out to me as I played on the front porch diaperless.

"PeepO! PeepO!"

I would dip down between the rails of the porch and squint at her then run inside laughing as she threatened, "That butterfly will fly away if you don't put your diaper back on!"

But those were the days when the whole world belonged to me, before Desiree and then Mary. Mary was being tickled now, on her chubby belly, and rubbed with soft fingers on the hard gums that Elizabeth said were breaking teeth.

Desiree and I ran off back down the yard, chasing each other under the house, playing Catcher pass the farm gate and through to the meadow with the smell of sea breeze and cow dung and sheep dung and fat flies buzzing and marabuntas crazy for our town skin and us both crazy for all this space; no longer hemmed into our own yard surrounded by houses and neighbours looking down through their windows or from their front steps minding your business or what you were wearing or who was coming in your front gate or if your Daddy was still up the river and your Mummy gone to Matinée again?

Aunty Carmelita had started cooking and the smell of onions and spices and frying chicken came curling into the yard.

"Girls!" she shouted, "Girls! Foodings time! Fetch you Daddy and Uncle Beau!"

The men were tinkering with the old Chevy. Uncle Beau had told Daddy that he "got the real stuff upstairs, man", and they were knocking back glasses tinkling with ice and holding golden liquid that soon disappeared down their throats, and even as we watched, the ice melted, and our favourite uncle and our Daddy held their glasses in cupped hands and scratched their heads at the same time staring at the open car bonnet with its engine curled up inside like a dead snake. And the cries came from the house again.

"Beau! Jim! What y'all doing so? And where those girls gone, the food getting cold!"

"Elizabeth," Aunty Carmelita said, when we'd eaten all the dinner up and everybody was sitting on the porch, "Elizabeth, this time I gon be real careful, this time things gon go well fuh true." And Uncle Beau say how much he love his Carmelita and no baby would make him love her any more, is she he want, and after all the sad losses, well...Then they remembered we were there and sent us off to play downstairs. The hum of their voices reached us through the floor of the veranda as we played on the leather seat of the blue Chevy, me at the wheel, Aunty Carmelita crooning to Mary, Mummy slapping sandflies, Uncle Beau's wide cowboy laugh dropping like the night through the wide floorboards.

There are times for stories, and there are times for *stories*. When night has fallen and the air is filled with the croaking of crapauds and the creaking of rockers, when the radio has been turned off for the day and the only light is the oil lamp swinging from the hook, when the children are tired of the day but not yet ready for bed, that is the time for stories, that is the time for jumbies. That is the time for family stories, falling from the lips of mothers and grandmothers staving off the fears of the night. My mother was told no stories as a child. She had one storybook, a book of rhymes whose pages she turned again and again. But stories came. They came through dreams, they came through the living, they came through the dead. For her too, they would come through *True Life* magazines, the radio, and the movies.

From the lips of the storytellers they have always fallen, linking settlements between long roads, and even longer nights. They have helped to make the world smaller, and even as footsteps disappear traces remain. When pen fell on paper and cable lines ran under the sea, stories ran too, written stories, coming in through the radios, keeping 1950s housewives alert and needing. And there are stories that are not meant for the ears of children, that are half-signed, or whispered with an ear to the door.

They come, as bold as brass and bright as day, not caring about the ears of children. Came from one cast off as women were, one whose bitterness caused her to carry poisoned apples. And one such climbed on the Rosignol train that day to wag her fingers into the face of a grandmother, and pour the future into her ear. Tell them, tell them, the story maker says, that the belly might catch but the fruit will remain on the tree.

And early one morning in May 1961, when I was seven years old, I woke up to the sound of Mummy and Daddy's voices in the dining room. It was still dark. I rubbed my eyes, and climbed over Des, padded across the bedroom floor and opened the door. Daddy was sitting at the dining table having breakfast, and Mummy was pouring him coffee. Mummy's belly was big; she was having another baby, the one we had screamed at the aeroplane for, jumping up and down on the bridge, "Aeroplane aeroplane bring us a baby sister," and who will arrive in August, and this makes her move slowly.

"Where are you going, Daddy?" I ask, thinking, he is going to the river and will be away for days. But my parents look at each other, and I can see their eyes are red.

"We'll have to tell her," Mummy says, "they'll have to know sometime."

"Tell me what?" I was suddenly wide awake.

Mummy sat on the dining chair and pulled me onto her lap.

"It's your Aunty Carmelita," she says slowly, stroking my hair. Her voice is hoarse and I am suddenly afraid.

"Aunty Carmelita is...is gone, Margaret."

"Gone? Gone where?"

"She's gone to heaven."

Gone to heaven? That place in the clouds with Jesus who you couldn't really see? I grow cold. I don't want Aunty Carmelita to go where I can't see her.

I stamp my feet and holler, not *my* Aunty Carmelita with her brown eyes laughing playing peepso through the banister rails. What does Jesus want with her? NO. NO. NO. *You're fibbing! You're telling stories! It's not true!* I turn to Daddy, who is quiet, and who is holding his head in his hands.

*Let me go Daddy, let me go too.* I want to see my Aunty Carmelita, want to see her...But Mummy holds me back by the front door and I watch my Daddy climb down those front steps, go, catch the boat, go to Georgetown, go to Aunty Carmelita's *fineral*. Aunty Carmelita who went to Heaven trying to have a baby. As I got older I heard of the babies she had conceived and lost, baby after baby. The last one took her. My mother dreamed her. She, Elizabeth, was walking down a long road and came to a large white house surrounded by beautiful gardens. There was my Aunty Carmelita, looking up from the garden, her face breaking into a smile. *Elizabeth! O Elizabeth I am so pleased to see you!* And she invited her in, showed her around the roses and the frangipani, the oleander and bougainvillea. And there were the beautiful babies all gathered around her. *She was with her children*, my mother said. And stood waving and waving from the garden gate until my mother turned the corner.

My sister Yonnette was born that August, after months of me and my sisters standing on the bridge yelling at every aeroplane that passed overhead. That was how babies came, we'd been told. She came screaming in just like a jet plane, bald-headed and red-faced, and was promptly named after Yonnette D'Andrade, the announcer on Radio Demerara. I was pleased to see she had blue eyes; at last somebody matched up with me.

# 11

# Schooldays, Early

To my first teacher, a memory – You sit me on your lap because I'm small. I haven't yet fit in. I haven't yet begun to learn to settle at my desk and chair, to watch the board and you, to be still. I cry for Home. Something about me has touched you. You shush me up and hush the class and place me on your lap. I settle back against you, thumb in mouth. The room is big and strange, all those faces staring. My fingers search for comfort; my blanket isn't here, some silky anything to pluck and whisper in-between my fingers. But your blouse is smooth. My fingers stop at buttonholes, soft, cloth-covered buttons where soft threads slip between my searching fingers. I lay back in my dreaming, the warm drone of your voice a rhythm on my ribs. Then, I am wobbling on the classroom floor, my thumb a gap between my lips. You shout:

"You nasty-minded little girl! I give you some attention and look what you gone and do! Rip off my shirt button! Jesus give me faith. G'wan, g'wan! Back! Siddown in your seat!"

Roman School playground, all brown uniforms and white shirts. The children are playing a ring game and the person in the middle is trying to break out between the tight clasp of fingers. She leans on them with all her strength.

"You think ah cyant break it?"

"No koloka!"

"Whuh kinda game this?"

I stand on the outside watching. I've played this game before in my own street; I can almost feel the fingers digging into my palm. But I haven't been invited to join in this game.

The breaker breaks through, and a cheer goes up, I can't help myself, a smile is hovering on my lips. The girl who's just been outed notices.

"Whuh you skinning yuh teeth for, Anita Harris?"
*Why do they call me Anita? That's my second name.*
I can feel my skin grow cold, the sun crawl and hide in my belly. All the other children turn and look at me. I hang back against the fence.

Some suck their teeth and cut their eyes on my skin; the looks cut sharp like razor grass.

Then somebody else says, " Leave she nuh."

Eyes swing back to the circle where a new breaker cries, "You think ah cyant break it?"

"No koloka."

"Whuh kinda game this?"

"Awee game this."


In 1963 we are moved next door to the convent school; my Daddy wants the best for his girls. This is where the sons and daughters of Lawyer This and Doctor That and the gold-haired children from the sugar estates go. We wear Carmelite brown pinafores.

We're lined up on the concrete path, off to the Gaiety Cinema. The Sisters have arranged us in threes, and walk up and down the line warning us to behave with silence and dignity. There's to be no idle chattering, no stepping out of line. I don't know the names of the girls in my line. They won't even smile at me. I lean forward. Can I see Desiree? There she is, right at the front. She's looking back too. My eyes fill up with tears.


In the classroom with the trellis they are showing us pictures of people called communists who don't love The Lord and will go to Hell. In the picture the Holy Bibles are piled high in the street and the communists have torches in their hands which they raise high above their heads like flags. People are running. There is something called a tank too in the picture, a big car with a big gun, with a small man inside it and big wheels like tractor's. This makes me feel afraid. We're told to pray for the souls of the communists who don't know what they're doing.

\* \* \* \* \*

With two schools side by side, before school call-in the noise is like a flock of parakeets as they're getting ready to roost. Then bells ring and whistles sound and the doors swallow all the children up; whispers are stubbed out in hallowed halls where children are seen but must not be heard. Latecomers huff and puff in the heavy scent of Mansion Polish and bowls of roses placed before Our Lady. School shoes squeak, and a clock chimes the hour, anxious for the Angelus, the glory of the day. Sister walks between the desks with her ruler, inspecting our fingernails, rapping knuckles. Then it's bowed heads, prayers and lessons. Her chalk scrapes the blackboard; our chalk scratches on our slates. A knock on the door and in glides Reverend Mother. We rise like a wave, chairs scraping as everyone rises and sings all together:

"Good Morning Reverend Mother."

Interrupting the warm morning come milk and orange juice, break-time, run-in-the-school-yard time, run-close-to-the-fence time as Roman School children stick out their tongues surreptitiously at us through the fence.

Needlework time. Sister Ambrose's room will forever be daisy stitches. Here time will fly for me. At first clumsy thumbs and fingers handle squares of fabric, eyes squint at needles, teeth tempt thread. Then my fingers are set free, the dance begins, thoughts whirr at speed, immersing themselves into the slick rhythm of needle, thread, thumb, forefinger, looping between fabric and air, broken only by knots which mouth descends to bite in temper. Sister's soft voice, "Scissors." Getting caught in a tangle time, daisy petal all wrong and bunched. Sister's tough thumbs coaxing...

"Unpick and start again. More haste less speed, child."

Perfect petal unfolding, uncurling between fabric and forefinger, primrose with lilac centre, green ivy stems creeping towards endless perimeters. I wouldn't hear the bell, just my breath and the ticking clock. The sudden scrape of chairs makes me jump. Other eager girls rise up, replace, fold away. Be done; leave.

"Margaret, you can go now," Sister Ambrose says, but the chair holds on to the back of my knees, releasing me unwillingly with a sticky, impatient sigh.

The lunch boxes belonging to the sugar estate children sit on the ledge beneath the window. Sandwich boxes some of us have never seen the like of, filled with muffins, chocolate cake, fancy biscuits from Booker's. The boys have bristling blond hair and athletic knees. Their faces are like apples, flushed sorrel-red, deep bronze. The girls' pencil cases sing of other places: Big Ben and Niagara Falls, Disney World and New York skyscrapers. Freckles dance across their faces. They had Other, Away lives; America and Canada lives; English lives with cousins and aunts and grandparents with whom they spend Vacation. Their parents are estate managers, overseers, economic advisors.

As yet I have not visited either Blairmont or Albion Estate. I know only that Blairmont is across the river, next to Rosignol, and Albion winds its mysterious way inland off the Corentyne highway. The estate children are a group of otherness. They move with an ease I can only dream of, have a magic dust that ignites the smiles of the nuns, speak of The Pool in which they can't wait to take a dip when they get home. Lucky is the child who is invited to visit. Those that do are already privileged, part of a private club. Many of these children have one or other parent from abroad who has married a Guyanese; others are so close to the church you can smell the incense. Sayings pepper out: *some o' dem more white dan de white people demself. She ain nobody, plain simple nurse-girl from Birmingham or London marry awee boys studying for doctor or lawyer. Loneliness musee ketch dem, or dem like white wimmin bad. Dem come back swinging pon dem arm and before you know it dem think dem queen with servant an ting.* They accompany their parents to the Catholic Men's Club and learn to swim, play piano and dance ballet. The bright yellow school bus is waiting for them when the school doors open at 1pm, and they clamber aboard swinging their lunch boxes while those others like me disperse across New Amsterdam to tables waiting with plates of chowmein or saltfish and rice, hassa curries and pepperpot, beef stew and squash, cook-up rice. My main envy is ballet: legs up on the windowsill for a barre, perfect pirouettes practiced with the cats...ballet is not within our budget or heritage. Decades later I will join a class and be told what a shame I wasn't trained, I would have made such a good dancer...

Faces had, over the past couple of years, begun to individualise.

There were de Souzas, Annamanthodos, Mohabirs, Girdharrys, Diyaljees, Fung-a-fooks, and Gomes.

At the same time I am realising that I am not particularly bright. I can read, and write; I can recite. I like to draw. I have an interest in stories and other cultures and countries. But my grasp of anything mathematical comes limping in. I struggle with homework and Elizabeth tries to help but gets cross with me. I even lie to Sister once that I forgot my homework. She calls my bluff, sending me home to get it, as we only live across Main Street. I cry and cry at home but Mummy sends me back. Some of the children get top marks all the time. They are heading for Berbice High School; you need to pass Common Entrance for that! There is doubt that I will. But in the playground other battles are fought daily: who is friends with whom, who wants to sit next to whom, who has been invited to so-and-so's party, whose mother has been invited to bridge or the whist drive at so-and-so's house. Our Common Entrance Class, with its newly-aware ten and eleven-year-olds, caught between *fastness* (curiosity) and fear of Sister, wanted to see what a nun's room looked like.

The interior walls of the convent, like all the buildings in British Guyana, didn't reach the ceiling; hot days and wooden houses called for fretwork panels, lattice-work between the top of the wall and the ceiling which welcomed the breeze and aimed at keeping thief man out. Our class was at the top of the building, on the same floor as the Sisters' bedrooms, and it was easy enough to take advantage of their absence one morning and pull a desk and chair close to the wall.

The nuns intrigued and awed us. They glided soundlessly across the hall. Their faces glowed from the hoods of their chocolate brown veils; the rosary beads from their waists oscillated against each other, distinctive shines competing, onyx, glass and silver, mother-of-pearl.

Sister Jeanne, Sister Ambrose, Sister Rose, Sisters Joseph and Jacinta.

Even in their sternness, even in my fear of them, I thought them beautiful. Even as discipline, passion, retribution and fear of God blazed from their glances like lances, falling on some and not on others.

At home, in our bathroom mirror I arranged a towel around my features; perfectly oval, if not symmetrical. What a sense of belonging I felt, how beatific. When I grew up I was going to be a Sister too, and glide along those gleaming corridors, a Bride of Christ.

Brides of Christ: what did that really mean? What was that passion that propelled young girls to leave families from islands and continents far across the sea, all the way from Ireland and Nova Scotia, Canada and Portugal, Africa?

We couldn't imagine their bodies, or their lives before this one. When lovely Sister Jacinta laughed with us and told us about her family in Trinidad we realised that under her habit breathed a young girl less than ten years older than we were. Did they *choose* this life? Did they *want* it? I heard it said in Portuguese families right there in New Amsterdam, as they remarked on the separate characteristics of their housefuls of sons and daughters:

"This one's for Our Lord."

And in church I remember thinking, blasphemously, as I watched those handsome altar boys gliding with chalice in hand, *not that one, Lord.*

What would the nuns' bedroom look like? Gossip pinged between myself, Lorna, the twins and Rome. So we peeped over in turn, with someone as lookout.

"What can you see? What can you see?"

It was so spartan we could not believe it. There was Sister's narrow bed, a simple bedspread, a blanket folded neatly, a small bedside table with a Bible and a mosquito coil, a brown wardrobe.

Nothing else.

No mirror, no pictures on the wall, no radio.

No mirror!

In front of the bathroom mirror at home, with the towel wrapped round my face, I would try to imagine life without a mirror. Would open my eyes slow enough to try and catch myself with my eyes shut. To the strange sight of my flat nose and fat-lipped cat-eye features.

No hairbrush, no clothes left on a hanger.

No rows of shoes under the bed.

No mirror.

We had just begun to style our own hair, investigating the possibilities of creations beyond the ponytail or pigtail.

Mummy sat at her dressing table brushing out her soft brown hair from the curlers, fixing a kiss curl on the side of her cheek. Mary would emerge looking cute with perfect plaitlets, Desiree with her ribbon bows, and Yonnette's white-blonde head shone like a hatchling.

"They haven't got any hair, remember," one of the girls said. "They have to shave it off for marrying Christ."

And that thought was the worst thing, those beautiful faces crowned, under their veils, by a halo of fuzz. And when we went to see *The Nun's Story*, which was sold as a must-see because it had nuns in it and the beautiful Audrey Hepburn, and (I suspect) the story of 'savage' Africa; nothing stirred us more than that scene when Hepburn's hair is shorn, and falls, dark and lovely, all about her. That image, and the one of her splayed full out on the floor in front of the altar, filled us with horror: imagine leaving your family and friends and travelling right across the world with an invisible bridegroom for the beautiful sacrifice of an eternal life without hair.

**12**

# Passing

The parrots are screaming. Could be they are challenging someone's escaped bird come to join them? You see them sometimes, enjoying their liberty in the treetops, bright feathers red against the green. They think they're hidden, settling in the branches amongst the leaves, but their racket makes that a lie. Mad birds, sticking their heads out as if someone's come to their front door.

Sometimes the coconut boy shins up the tree to try and catch one, but they're not stupid, even the so-called tame ones. They wait till he's almost beneath the branches, then fly off laughing, leaving him throwing stones and swearing.

"Scunts! Parrot rasses! Ah gon boil you fuh true!"

When Mother and Daddy J come down to town they bring their parrot Polly, who sits on the front porch as if she owns it. Her walk along the rail looks like those drunks making their way home from Betty's Bar. She can screech even louder than those birds up there.

"Mother! Mother! Where Mother gone? Mother!" she screams. She cocks her head on the side, looking at us.

"Mother gone?"

This was such a morning. Parrots screeching, the kiskadees answering back, radios playing, neighbours' voices loud over the back fence.

I was playing the 'pretend we've got a record player' game, turning the radio up loud and holding Daddy's old 78s up to the gallery window at intervals. I wasn't allowed to use the radiogram; but the girls across the road, plaiting each other's hair on their front steps, didn't know that. And the hits coming from Radio Paramaribo were just too cool to miss: The Beach Boys, The Beatles, The Cats. The synchronisation was going well: turn the volume button down when the Dutch announcer's voice came on, lift the record sleeve up to the window, squint at the writing, hold two records up even, as if it was difficult to choose between

The Hollies and The Dave Clark Five. They were not close enough to see that it was actually The Best of the Merrymen or The Tijuana Brass. If cut-eye could kill, I could have died a thousand times. It wasn't *my* fault I went to the convent, or that my daddy's bottom didn't hang over his bicycle seat, and actually he wouldn't be on his motorbike for much longer, we were gonna get a pick-up truck soon, yeah man.

Rover was barking and barking as the postman cycled up. The postman rung his bell and shouted *Harris!* up at the window. I leaned out, record sleeve in hand. He was pushing his cap off his forehead, wiping the sweat off.

"Don't just stare out the window at me girl!" he snapped. "Come and get y'all letters, I'm not passing that mad dog!"

Elizabeth flip-flopped to the front door.

"Margaret, you exam results must be come."

She stood by the front door and watched me run down the stairs. Rover was straining at the lead, his teeth bared like Dracula, spit dropping out of his mouth, his one eye fixed fast on the postman. He had always followed Elizabeth to the cinema, even though she would turn round and chase him back. He would hang back and hide then run after her again. No surprise then, that Saturday afternoon when, blinded by his pursuit, he charged across Water Street and a car came straight and knocked him down. That's how he lost his eye. Since then my sweet-natured pet had got bad-tempered. Even after I had thrown him out the window all that time ago he'd never got this bad. He'd even growl at me now when I went to feed him.

"Don't put your face near to him," Daddy warned. "Don't ever take his bowl away when he still eating."

If we let him off the chain, he bounded straight over the gate and chased everybody who came past on a bicycle, causing them to lift their knees up to the handlebars as they tried to freewheel past the Harris mad dog.

The postman remained seated on his bike, and passed me the letters through the gate.

He sucked his teeth and said, "That's a nasty dangerous dog y'all got there! You better watch somebody don't poison he!"

Elizabeth held out her hand as I came back up the steps.

"Come give me! Give! You Common Entrance result come?"

She was more excited than I was. I stood there wordless, trying not to think. My mother flicked through the mail, muttering "damn light bill already," then pulled out a brown envelope.

"Here it is!" She made the sign of the cross swiftly. "Lord see fit to bless this child. Amen."

"THIS IS RADIO PARAMARIBO BRINGING YOU THE HITS!"

The radio announcer's voice blared through the window and the girls across the road burst out laughing. Elizabeth had pulled out a white sheet of paper and was scrutinising it.

"Margaret, for God sake turn down that blasted radio!"

I dashed inside, more because of the sniggering than her command. As I reached for the dial Mummy screamed.

"You passed! You passed! Come here child, let me bless you."

She gathered me close in a tight squeeze and dropped hot kisses on the top of my head.

"You see? All that studying helped! The Good Lord helped you. Didn't I tell you the Lord helps those who help themselves?"

My mind flashbacked to the last year. Homework nights. Elizabeth sitting at the dining table with me, going over and over again sums that meant nothing. She would have the ruler ready, to hit me across the knuckles or the arm. I was all right with spelling, with comprehension, with drawing, but sums? If I passed anything it was down to the Lord indeed, and Elizabeth's prayers.

She went back to reading the letter and I leant over her shoulder.

"What's the difference between 'qualify' and 'pass'?"

"It means you've passed but you might not have passed high enough to get a place at Berbice High. Go and get dressed, and we'll go and see the Headmaster, Mr Beharry. We'll stop and tell Tita on the way."

So stupid ole me had passed.

Stupid ole me who more and more felt dunce and clumsy. Send me to find something and I couldn't find it. Put me at a tennis table and I could neither serve nor return the ball. I would always come last at anything that involved physical activity. Except for skipping: lining up in the street to jump in just at the right moment, rope whacking the newly laid tarmac, lifting dust, two girls turning, six hands clapping, and all the chants that went with it: *one, two, three, four, five, will you marry me, marry me, get baby.*

And hula hoops...one, two, even three, yellow, blue, pink or red, my bony hips would trap them there circling and circling to Kingdom Come till Mrs So-and-So would lift her eyebrow and tell Elizabeth:

"That is certainly a Madam you're raising there."

But hula hooping, skipping, drawing and losing yourself in stories don't pass exams, so it had to be Mummy's prayers, luck, or a blind examiner. I thought back to the exams, which seemed a long time ago now. All the schools had had to go to Vryman's Erven on the Backdam to sit the Common Entrance. I remembered the cut-eyes from the children from the other schools. Unfamiliar stairs, unfamiliar classrooms, windows looking out over the Backdam. There were no boys swimming in the trench, no kites flying; just a hot room, an exam paper, no talking, a teacher *invigilating.*

Wallace taught me to fly kites there, after we'd made them with sticks and kite-paper from Daniel's shop.

"Run! Run!"

And though running was never my thing, not now that everybody was starting to laugh at my skinny legs, off I went, like the wind.

"Run!" Wallace said.

And he'd hold the tail high till the wind caught the kite and lift she would lift, sing she would sing, fly she would fly till she ran head first into a jamoon tree.

Elizabeth was chattering away as we got ready to go out that Saturday morning.

"We'll have to write and tell all your uncles and auntys in Georgetown. You might get a small piece! I wonder if Alex passed? He might go to Queens! I hope Mr Beharry will let you in to Berbice High..."

She creamed her face, patted on face powder, then lipstick and eyebrow pencil.

She made a face in the mirror, sucked her lips in, dabbed them with a piece of toilet paper.

"Thank the Lord you didn't fail! Lord knows what school you'd have had to go to then!"

The sun's already high in the sky when we step out. Elizabeth's forgotten it's my turn to do the front steps. Her perfume has rivals, the roses, the frangipani, all pouting their lips up to the sun. The girls across the road are still plaiting each other's hair.

Elizabeth smiles up at them. "Morning girls. Your Mummy home? I got some good news for her!"

"Morning, Mrs Harris. No, Mummy gone to market already."

"Oh all right, I'll see her later."

I nudged her in the ribs.

"Don't tell them!" I hissed.

For once she listened.

"Come let's tell Tita, we have to tell her first or she'll be vexed."

I felt stupid, remembering my childhood disgrace at the bottom of Tita's steps to the Wife of the Manager of the Royal Bank of Canada. Imagine lifting my skirt and showing a white lady my panty! Tita (Daddy's sister Emily) was strict too. She would make me and Desiree sit, *Knees together, palms on laps, like little ladies*. If we chattered too much she would put a finger on her lips and say, "Quiet speech is a mark of refinement."

Her house was stuffed with antiques, dark polished furniture with curved arms and rattan insets. There were doilies on top of everything, and large Victorian brass pots holding palms. There was a lot of brass which we girls were sent over to polish once a week as *the devil makes work for idle hands*; long oblong boxes which had no apparent use except to be polished, laid into with all our might, with Brasso and a yellow cheesecloth duster. Spoons too; solid silver ladles with curved handles which we rubbed until they could see our faces. The glass cabinet was full of china which was never used. Tita's husband, Mr Westmoreland, had died years and years ago, and they never had their own children. Tita still wore calf-length old-fashioned dresses, of the type that

Evelyn was wearing in that photograph way back in the thirties, and this was 1965.

One thing I loved best in Tita's house was the love-seat. That chair for two, seats facing opposite directions, carved arms in solid mahogany, *Jamaica wood*. Desiree and I would sit, under the stern eyes of Mr Westmoreland, pretending to be lovers. I was the suitor come to call, my sister the girl, sitting knees together and palms up, eyes cast demurely on the floor. As we polished I quoted the latest verse I had learnt at school: *fair maid, my heart's ease*, keeping an ear out for Tita tinkling crockery in the dark backroom kitchen. We dissolved in giggles halfway through, Tita's voice trickling out of the kitchen: "Laugh if you're laughing, cry if you're crying."

I glanced up at the windows. Tita would be more than thrilled to hear the news. But the morning was getting on.

"Let's tell her when we get back," Elizabeth said, "I want to see Mr Beharry, and I still have to go to market."

Water Street was busy as usual, with Saturday morning traffic from the country, car horns blowing, buses spewing out diesel fumes. A donkey cart was holding up the traffic outside Barclays Bank, the driver taking his time, ignoring the car drivers shouting "Give that jackass two good lash nuh man!"

Elizabeth stopped to talk to a million people. This was something I hated: my mother and New Amsterdam's ceaseless capacity for conversation; children being made to stand under the burning sun and yakking that circled the universe. The only frisson of interest was when their voices dropped and the phrase *well you know that little ears are sharp but*...and that's the way you heard who wore a shocking mini to church even though she was pregnant and how Betty's rumshop was harbouring too many that should come straight home and how beauty queens were only chosen for their high colour.

Now that there was news to tell it was worse.

My passing was *a vision of the future. Without education we are nowhere and nothing child. The only way to move forward in this life. You must make you mummy and daddy proud of you.*

Silver was taken out of pockets and purses and laid in my hand. *Walk good, child, by the grace of the Lord.*

The sun was beating down on the top of my head, and by the time we stopped in the shade of the market to tell Ruby's mother the news, I was glad of the shade.

On the way back we stopped in Fung Fook's grocery store to place our weekly grocery order. The boy Ten Choy would bring it later, a cardboard box full on the front of his delivery bike, ring his bell at the back gate. The smell of the spices hit your nose from outside on the pavement: curry powder, garam masala, cinnamon and cloves, all-spice and ginger, coffee beans. The boy was helping behind the counter weighing and wrapping, sliding the ladder sideways to reach the top shelves. Elizabeth handed over her list and was just starting to ask if he'd passed his exam too when all of a sudden there was a commotion at the door and Elizabeth heard her name being shouted.

"Mrs Harris here? Mrs Harris! Oh God..."

Ruby stood breathless in the doorway. She bent her head down to catch her breath, her hands on her thighs, then straightened up and began to fan herself agitatedly with her hands. The shoppers waiting at the counter turned their heads.

"Mrs Harris, Oh God Mrs Harris..."

"Ruby! What in God's name is the matter girl?" A cloud dropped down over her face. "Is one of the children...?"

Ruby's face was all twisted, the words all jumbled up as she shook her head. "No, no, the children all right...Oh Mrs Harris, bad trouble come..."

The grocer came round from the counter with a glass of water.

"Girl, easy, easy, you gon give yourself a heart attack. Now tell we slowly is what happen."

"Is you sister-in-law..."

"Mrs White?"

"No, the other one..."

"Tita? What happen to her Ruby, what?!"

One word burst out.

"Fire!"

"What? The house?" Elizabeth crossed herself. "Jesus Lord!"

"Mrs Westmoreland lean over the kerosene stove…"

Tears were streaming out of Ruby's eyes. "She lean over in her long nightie and…Oh Lord Mrs Harris, I don't know how to tell you this…she burn up bad-bad!"

"Oh God, no."

Elizabeth grabbed my hand and ran out of the shop, her small feet in her slingback shoes half-running, half-walking as swiftly as they could along Main Street. I can see her now in her shift dress, her market basket in her hand. Ruby following, keeping pace, filling her in as much as she could between her short shallow breaths. I heard about smoke blowing out of Tita's window, and Tita running out on the porch, her hands trying to beat down the flames that were blazing from her nightie. But Tita was old, and couldn't move fast, or shout loud enough…and the fire had burn up she nightie faster than she hands could beat it down…

My heart had begun to hammer like my feet on the pavement. Oh dear Gentle Jesus, if only we had gone in there first…

Ruby kept forcing out more words like *fire engine* and *ambulance* and *hospital*.

I never even heard the fire engine! When did it come screaming past? When we were busy knocking at Mr Beharry's door? Strolling round the market? How long had we been out? An hour? Two? Time was all mixed up: with the sun high overhead it felt like midday; but only just now I'd been singing along to the Beach Boys and Elizabeth had been opening my exam envelope. Only just now I was taking the envelope from the postman and Rover was straining from his chain baring his teeth like a mad dog.

How can your world change so fast? Our feet beat on the pavement, a sound that seemed louder in my ears than all the car horns blowing as we carelessly crossed roads and headed towards St John Street. When we got to the top, the fire engine was still there, spraying water up Tita's front steps and her door.

The ambulance had taken her already.

Neighbours were gathered round the front gate, parting as

we came though. Some of them put out their hands and patted Mummy.

"So sorry Mrs Harris, what a thing! What a thing!"

Desiree was standing on the porch, her face white and long as a pot spoon, her grey eyes like water. She ran downstairs, put her arms around Mummy, and started to cry.

"I saw her Mummy, I saw her through the window..."

"Don't upset yourself little Des. I better fly to the hospital."

"I saw her face in the ambulance...I was looking down through the gallery window..."

"Come, let's go inside."

Tita died later that night. Daddy came home from the hospital and sat in the dark in the gallery chair a long long time. Before I fell asleep I remembered, we'd never got to tell Tita I'd passed.

# 13

# Corentyne Tales: 2

Excitement isn't the word. We run round like the marabuntas Daddy smoke out from under the house. Hunting for swimsuits and sandals, getting in Mummy's way as she tried to pack the picnic basket. The Georgetown cousins have come and they're taking everybody to 63 beach. Well everybody except Mary and Yonnette because there isn't enough room in the car plus it's too hot for Yon-Yon. Mary is crying her eyes out but she has to help Ruby with her little sister. "And anyway you can go back with Aunty and Uncle for a whole week in GT, how's that!" Elizabeth says.

But, cry, cry, cry like Rainstorm.

Me and Alex argue all the time. He is too tall, he is too handsome, he is too smart-alec with his Georgetown city boy ways, always teasing.

Des fights me for the window seat. She, as usual, wants to sit on Mummy's lap, but I got there first, and wedge my bottom securely between her knees.

"Is not fair!" Desiree wails.

"Let your sister have a turn nuh," Elizabeth says.

"No," I say firmly.

The bridge is up at Canje and we wait in the line of traffic.

The river runs inland, heading for the canefields. We crane our necks to see the ship coming through. Uncle is talking about Booker's, where he works, and sugar, and about how the sugar goes all the way from here to the Demerara docks, and then to Tate & Lyle in England where they make it into small white cubes. I am only half listening. I'm watching the ship as it cuts oddly through the line of cars and buses and the tall steel fingers of the bridge.

"What's wrong with we brown sugar?" Desiree pipes up.

"Nothing at all dear," Aunty says. "People do a lot of strange things in this world."

"Hmm," Uncle grunts, "if they didn't we wouldn't be driving this car!"

Elizabeth and Aunty raise their eyebrows and smile at each other over our heads. Then the bridge drops down and we move off, passing through all those villages with the names I like: Palmyra, Albion, Fyrish...

When we pass Albion Estate, I turn my head to watch the long road branching off the highway, curving like a camoodi into the darkness of coconut trees, thick bush, cane.

In one of his rare moments Daddy J once told us a story about a white Dutchman he'd seen waiting on Albion Bridge. Only he didn't know it was a ghost till he passed. It was just a white man wearing a straw hat, and Daddy J said he should have known really, because the man had tipped his hat and said *Good Morning* as Daddy passed and white men didn't do that to black men then; so when Daddy J turned round and looked back only to see Nobody standing there, it was there and then he knew. But he wasn't frighten, he said, there's more to frighten from the living than the dead.

That was where the white children from school lived, where their yellow bus took them after they'd piled in with their red knees and lunch boxes talking about how hot it was, and how they couldn't wait to cool down in the pool.

When the car passed Williamsburg, Elizabeth got excited, leaning forward in her seat to see the house where she'd grown up.

It stood there unchanged, shutters facing the road, gallery windows whispering to me the memories of playing the Uncle game, of me and Des helping in the shop, and poor Charles the donkey lying dead in the back yard.

The highway shimmered ahead of us. Old plantation houses rose from wide meadows, white galleries flickering through the wide leaves of trees and the drunken angles of coconut palms. New concrete houses had been inserted into the landscape: businessmen and lawyers building palaces in the Corentyne breeze. The colours echoed the blue of the sky and jewelled the skyline with fluorescent pinks and luminescent oranges.

This is rice country, sugar-cane country. Great sheets of paddy dry on the flat concrete forecourts of farms. Small flurries of smoke signal where somebody burning bush. Cattle and sheep ignore the passing traffic. A cow lies dead by the side of the road. Away over yonder the Corentyne River goes about its business.

63 Beach always seems so far. My thighs got so sticky Elizabeth pushed me forward off her lap, and stuck her head out the window catching the breeze.

"Sixty miles," Daddy said.

People along this East Coast road walked miles to fetch water in the dry season; Elizabeth was saying how she and Uncle used to walk three miles to school in ninety-eight degrees heat.

The houses thinned out as we drove further into the country, smoke curling from the bottom of dilapidated wooden houses where women squatted and stirred open stoves. Hammocks swung, dogs strained on their leads. *We nearly there yet?*

Who say Guyana ain got beaches? Kites were singing as the car bumped past the dunes. There was the hotel Mummy and Daddy stayed in on their honeymoon. We piled out of the car and hared off up and down the dunes, Alex and his long legs way in front, me temporarily forgetting running and me weren't friends. There was the ocean and all its promises, the Corentyne River running to meet it, and in the distance Nikerie, Dutch Guiana, vaporising in a heat haze.

*Three go to Nikerie...*How easy it was to imagine the periscope of a U-boat lurking out there in those waves, propelled by blond-haired men with cold blue eyes. The empty beach with its wind-twisted palms and creeping trunks stretched left and right as far as your eye could reach. Anything could land here at night and not be seen.

Aunty and Liz found a good spot, after surveying the entire horizon. Shade won, and under a silhouette of leaves triangled against the sun, they made a nest with rugs and picnic basket whilst Uncle strode purposefully towards the ocean drawing in big gulps of air. Jim was looking up at the wealth of coconuts, ripe and hanging low from the trees, and why the hell didn't he think of bringing his cutlass? Fresh coconut water! Geeze man!

We had our own coconut tree at home, *but that don't taste the same.*

"Never mind Jimbo," Aunty said. "You'll just have to

content yourself with a nice cool Banks' beer." She turned to Uncle, striding back to join the circle. "Honey?"

"Two women waiting on us! This is the life eh Jimbo!" He took the bottle and sprawled out on the sand.

I headed towards the water. I couldn't swim. Nor could Mummy. How could she? Where would she have learnt? New Amsterdam didn't have a pool, only the private one at CMC. The estate pools were by invitation only. The backdam trench was for boys; girls didn't do things like that. Daddy had learnt in the Berbice river, way back up there at Fort Nassau, though I was sure sure his sisters weren't allowed. Elizabeth couldn't even ride a bicycle.

My toes sank into wet sand. Alex was already in the water showing off, whooping and dashing head first into the surf. Of course he could swim. They went regularly to Palm Court and Kingston Pool in Georgetown. Not like his country cousins here. But this was *my* country, my big shot cousin didn't have any right to it! I glared at him and his antics. I looked back. Desiree was under the trees drinking lemonade. I felt naked and alone. The ocean was shining so. It sung, called like that story I'd heard about Fairmaids slipping out of the sea at night to converse with those who lived on land, that story I couldn't make any sense of yet, could not even make a fiction out of. I so wanted to be part of this ocean, enjoy it tumbling and unafraid like Alex, but didn't know how.

A large hand fell on my shoulder.

"Coming in little Meg?" Uncle kicked the waves with large hairy legs. "Come on, I'll teach you."

He held my hand and we walked deeper into the water. It was a cool balm to the burning sun and sand, the salt air and the glare stinging my eyes.

"Don't frighten darling, we'll stop here."

The rush of the waves was so strong they nearly knocked me over. I wobbled, and fell, awkward, clumsy, spurting, spitting water. The water was up to my waist. I watched the waves, prepared myself for the slam of them against me, braced myself for its childish runs, for the big ones.

"Dip your shoulders under now, just glide your arms about like this."

Uncle was behind me, strong and safe. I did as he said, getting used to the ripples, the feel of the push my arms gave. I looked back: a tiny Mummy, Aunty and Des were walking along the waterline. They looked further away than I'd thought. It unsteadied me, the look of them, the strange shift of the sand; I couldn't make out the tree under which Daddy stretched out. The skyline wobbled in the heat. I grew afraid. I was *outside* my country. For the first time I was looking at my country from *outside*.

The sand beneath seemed to dissolve. I slipped and fell, head under the waves, salt water in my mouth. I could see my uncle's feet through a blur.

I started to kick, moving my arms and legs under the water. I could feel myself moving past the anchors of his legs and broke the surface.

He was clapping his hands like a seal. "Good girl! Clever girl! Now let's see if you can do it *on top* of the water!"

Swimming? Was that swimming? I felt momentarily elated. But try as I might I couldn't do as he asked. All the time he watched I floundered till he got bored and swam off to join his son. I began to make my way back to the beach. With a last effort, checking that no-one was looking, I tried again. Lowered my body back into the water, eyes open. It seemed to remember, and started to propel itself. I had learnt to swim underwater.

# 14

# Kwakwani

Sailing on an ocean of brown water. Smooth, so smooth a passage. I can hardly feel a ripple. Daddy's at the wheelhouse and he waves as I turn to watch him, shading my eyes from the sun. I'm right at the front of the tug, *The Radio City,* chug chug away, little engine heart.

At night Daddy's boat cradles me, humming like a lullaby, rocking me into the arms of the river, tucked into the captain's bed underneath the mosquito net, a mosquito coil burning, the day disappearing into the fading calls of macaques and parrots; all those outside noises disappearing into the night.

In the daytime, the heat beats down on the barges; rust glints like copper, zinc and steel walkways burn right through my rubber slippers. The river swirls all around, miles of it; I can swing about with my arms outstretched and still it stretches away beyond the edges of my fingers.

We're chugging away from New Amsterdam, off to Kwakwani to fill up these four barges Daddy's tug is pushing like giant prams. Sometimes he steers close to the bank and I can see where ribbons of river slice away, race off behind bushes, to form creeks. Roots stick out of the water like antlers, logs and leaves, trees even, drifting and spinning past. Sometimes they look like alligators or manatees, and sometimes from the bank something moving turns out to be a canoe and somebody's arm is paddling fast-fast, cutting through the water left-right-left-right-left-right and Cook would shout as he threw out the fish bones and it could be somebody's cousin drawing up alongside with a letter to post or a parcel to pick up. And sometimes too another tug, *The Maracaibo* maybe, or *The Manhattan*, passed us, coming back from Kwakwani with its red hills of bauxite proud and pointed like Egyptian pyramids, and the sailors would throw words across the water, over the chug of the engines. *Their journey would be nearly done.* Soon those red hills would wait at Everton for a ship to take them way across the sea, where Reynolds would make them into Reynolds Wrap.

We can go faster when we're empty, and ride with the tide, and that's why, Daddy says, we have to wait for the tide, and why he leaves from home all those funny hours, when the sailor knocks on the door and says, "C'pn, sailing tonight at midnight."

I hang my head over the side and watch the water spit and gurgle between the barges and the tug, leaking blue oil, breaking into ripples, and I run to the stern to see the wake following us like a bridal train, glittering in the sunlight.

I liked to pretend I was a princess. I was the only girl onboard, and the sailors watched me, teased me, rubbed my hot head and warned me to keep out of the sun. This was *my* special trip, just me and Daddy; no Desiree, no Mary, no Yonnette. Daddy is different here; he never tells me off. I can lean right over the side till the spray touches my face, I can jump down and wander round inside the barges even; with *Matilda* in tow, I can play Hansel and Gretel, using the crumbs of bauxite to make a trail, but most of all, most of all, Daddy sometimes lets me hold the wheel and steer and even when the tug swings close to the bank, the barges jiggling up against each other, he easily rights it all, with fast, tight turns of hands whose veins ripple under his skin like worms.

When the sun comes down, the fireflies dance like the tips of the sailors' cigarettes, and the tilley lamp tilts, and the lights at the far ends of the barges look like stars in the darkness. The sailors liked to frighten me then, and tell tales of pumas and labbas, mongooses and snakes, plants that could bite you, swamps that suck you in, red ants as big as your thumb, spiders as large as your head, and mosquitoes and bats that drink your blood. They told jumbie stories of white men who got eaten up in the bush, and black men they used to chase, and how they're all still running around in there somewhere chasing each other even though they were dead and gone long time. They talked about Buck men too, saying how only Buck men knew bush; that's why they walked single file in town, but send one of them to catch you and you wouldn't get further than a spit. I never liked jumbie stories, or ole higue stories, especially here where there were so many trees for ole higues to hide in, trees which even though you couldn't see them in the blackness you know full well they travelling 'longside, creeping under the water with their big fat slimy mangrove feet, their coconut rot, their mash-up waterlog roots that spread all the way from here to Venezuela. Every spot of light from the far bank would make me move closer to Daddy, even though he told me that was only somebody house on the riverbank, not a ole higue waiting to enter a crack in the house and suck new baby blood. And when I went to bed, climbing up the short steel steps with my head full of jumbie and skeleton, I would check for holes in the mosquito net just in case one might find me, smell me and suck my blood like the bats I could hear chattering in the eaves at home; and my eyes would be peeling for the soft fall of those black velvet wings, or a ball of flaming light descending like a meteor and burning right through the mosquito net.

"Don't worry," the sailors laughed, "they only like babies, you too tough for them!"


Behind that thick bush the tug chugged past, did Grandfather Harris chop and slice, plant, hoe? Did Mama weed, pluck fowl, grow corilla, pound cassava, plait her children's hair with coconut oil? Where did they come from? Did the tracks I could see disappearing into the bush lead to the ruins of a plantation where Mama *Anna-Rose Boyle* and James Alexander grew up in the memory of massa's whip? What was Mama's Amerindian link? Where did the name Harris come from? Some plantation owner? Scottish, Welsh, English?

Daddy hardly told stories, apart from the one about drinking milk straight off a cow's bubby. Imagine that. I couldn't even imagine clearings big enough for canefields here; not that junglebush choke up – choke up like one splash of dark green shadow all along the waterline and curling thick into the sky full of *impenetrable bush*, anacondas, jaguars and jumbies, bark and branch and limb, monkey tails and tree frogs, and flowers hanging from the very tops of trees.

That strip of bush where white strips of sand gleamed across this water, stretching away into darkness, where in the daytime the tug passed women washing clothes, and children the size of thimbles jumped up and down waving; had my Daddy and Aunty, and Tita really live, eat, go to church, learn their lessons, ride horses there?

"We used boats the way you use your bicycle," he said once. And as the tug passed, the women and the children and the thin strip of sand would blend in with the trees and just disappear, so when I looked back all you could see was smudged watercolour green. Would I, if I had known, ever have built up the courage to ask, "Is fuh true Daddy, Bush swallow up your first wife so? And even after all this long long time Mummy's church don't believe she dead even though your English Church say seven years had passed, that's missing presumed dead, and that's why Mummy can't have Communion?"

But I wasn't supposed to know anything about things like that at all – at all.


Rosary beads roll between Angela's fingers. Mother-of-pearl from a riverbed deep in the Indian Ocean. Angela whispers an incantation in Greek which we repeat like parrots. We're developing a passion for the timbre of words, the rhythm and ripple of them. *Kyrie Eleison, Christe Eleison*...Mornings of masses have left ancient world languages tripping off our tongues although we know nothing of their meaning.


We are all travellers here. The altar, the candlelit room, the brass-locked, time-darkened chest of drawers, the iron bed...we've all sailed and creaked our way up the river. My grandparents' house has just three rooms; steps lead from the front porch down to the sandbank and a canoe. In the back porch rough wooden steps lead down to the vegetable garden and the latrine with its spiders and centipedes.

Another dark pit of hell with newspapers to wipe your bottom within earshot of the crackling, whistling jungle. The sound of the night creeps in through the shutters, coconuts crash onto the ground, branches rub up against each other, the canoe knocks against the jetty, the river sloshes up the sandbank.

During rainstorms, you feel there's a fight going on between jumbies and jungle, between the thunder and lightning, between the wind, water and sky; palm fronds and broken limbs of leaves fling themselves like missiles across the windows of my eyes. The river hurls itself with anger against the small canoe.

There are voices from the front porch and water slapping up the bank. The night is black-black. The fireflies dance round the kero-lamp. The rocking chair outside creaks and stops, creaks and rocks; Daddy J's pipe smoke wisps through the doorway. He is sipping his black ground coffee out there; black coffee made him black is what we're told. The smell lingers from the enamel pot on the stove from first thing in the morning.

Somebody had rowed in a canoe just before closing time. The shop was so close you could hear the thud of the paddle, the creak of the foot on the step. Daddy J had served him and now the voice was fading away, the cut of the paddle slicing the river, Daddy J and his coffee cup coming indoors. We'd hushed as he came in. Grace was said, and Amen, and the rattle of plates echoed Jack the capuchin's chain on the back porch as he ran back and forth, smelling food. That monkey was smart fuh true, and forever making us laugh with his antics. Take the belt round his waist. Jack could undo that belt whenever he felt the need. Undo it, run to the sugar barrel, lift the lid, scoop up a handful of sugar, replace the lid, then run back along the rail soon as he hears Mother coming; belt the belt back up, and rest his sharp brown eyes on the backyard, as if innocently admiring the scenery.

Yonnette was snivelling; the monkey had bitten her sharply earlier after he'd got fed up with Mary teasing him.

Yonnette's feet were not as fleet as her big sister's and Jack had caught her easy on her arm with his needle-sharp teeth. There had been a long debate about whether monkey bites were poisonous or not. Polly now, she liked nothing more than a debate. Danced along her cage upside down, pretended to cry like Yonnette, screaming *Jack!* and *Mother! Mother! Help! Help!* at intervals, and stuck her claws and red head out between the bars. Yonnette still has the scar.

Before bed we always had to say prayers; Daddy J read out of the black Bible, and Mother led the rosary, giving each of us a decade to recite. Then we all squeezed together in the big brass bed, lying crossways, whispering about the day and the night and the strangeness and the smells of earth and leaves, saltfish and tobacco and rain. The light from the lamp sneaked through the gap under the door, and shadows tossed left and right across the floorboards. We were a long way from home and streets and cars and buses.

Desiree and I were in the shop helping. We loved this; it reminded us of Williamsburg. It was even better than bush cook with Loretta or playing shop under the front steps at home, because people really came to buy things. We checked the tins of powdered milk, the packets of tea, the ground coffee; made a list for Mother. We'd made an entire three-piece set of dolls' furniture out of empty match and cigarette boxes. The shop counter faced the river, and we could see every customer as they turned their canoe or their speedboat into the gap, and would yell out to the back:

"Mother! Somebody coming!"

And it would be more than a purchase, this visit, it would be social too. Everybody wanted to know about *the grands come from town* and *what their name* and *how old you is?* This is the first place I see Amerindians easy in their home place, cutting through the water in dug-out canoes, *kreeyals*. Not like in town where people called them *bucks* in the same lowdown tone as they'd say *nigger, dutty putagee, coolie.*

\* \* \* \* \*

Mary and Yonnette play by the shoreline, digging with an old enamel cup and a calabash. Just where the rowing boat rests, all sorts of creatures hop and slide in and out of the mud. The mud makes a sucking sound as you dig, and fills up straight away with river water. Mary pats and moulds green mud pies and eats them. Really. Des and I are becoming separate entities from our younger sisters; they are *children*. We have no more time for mud pies, we say. Dollies are a different thing altogether. What I am actually doing is learning to sew. I have mastered Mother's treadle machine, and have run up a ball gown for Sindy, blue gathered skirt and halter top, satin cumberbund.

But nothing beats going out on the river itself, especially when Wallace lets us take turns at rowing. Round the sandbanks, ducking overhanging branches, dragging our hands over the side into the water which changes colour all the time, a line of silver where the sunlight rests, now red, now coffee.

"Up that way! Under there, Wallace!"

Damp fronds tickle the back of my neck.

"Paddle down there where it's dark and creepy! Who frighten? Me? No, boy!"

Canoe drifts into water black as armbands.

There is no silence such as this, where the sound of your own voice finds an echo which whispers right back at you, causing you to drop your oar, believing the creek to be alive and listening.

Kwakwani town, now.

Bouncing on top of the water, hoping the engine won't cut out. Watching out for the sandbank and that fast speedboat.

Slow where a tug's tied up alongside waiting.

There's even a handful of Her Majesty's soldiers lolling there by the wharf, their guns slung across their shoulders.

Up the concrete slope into town, just one road petering out, but there are the new houses, look, where Uncle Buggins and his wife and daughter Corinne live, and there's the commissary full of meat and fish and oil, sardines, flour, and those large tins of New Zealand butter, and small blue cubes for washing clothes and fishing line, and kerosene.

But the sun seems hotter here, the one main road dry and cracked in the heat, and already I'm longing for the journey back across that river that from as far back as I can remember drew a tight line right across my heart.

And then one day, some man is talking to me in the shop saying I'm a nice young lady and have lovely hair and eyes. He has laughter in his eyes. He comes back the next day and the next, and my hot ears start to listen for the sound of the outboard motor cutting out, and I'm brushing my hair smooth in front of Mother's vanity mirror.

And then one morning Daddy J shouts: "Get your tail in the kitchen and help your grandmother."

And he shouts at the man too, his voice moving outside saying, "Find somewhere else to buy your goods, there's nothing here for you!"

And the shame, and something more than shame, washes over all my body.

# 15

# St Rose's

*1965*

I'm standing back against the wall of the dark gym, waiting my turn to climb the ropes, vault the horse, brave the swing of my ponytail and the frizz of my fringe in the limelight, curl the indeterminate colour of my feet into new yachting shoes. In this gym I learnt all the songs from the Sound of Music, and briefly, briefly my voice broke free to dance like a butterfly against the panelled walls.

A year later I left my voice in Georgetown.

When, back home in New Amsterdam at the end of that school year, my mother sent me on an errand to Sister Jeanne, I stood at the convent door dumb, head hanging down, Sister waiting patiently for my words to break free.

I had left my voice in the dunce corner in the first form room at St Rose's, in my school desk, on the hockey field, in the house near Bourda Market, and in Brickdam Cathedral; buried it in the back seat of Baba's hire car, my father stern beside me, all the way from Bourda to Rosignol stelling.

The disappointment in Daddy's eyes as he stood on the doorstep of 'Aunt Lily's' had strangled any word that had wanted to offer utterance. Shame had settled on my shoulders. It had been a slow traveller, needing to comprehend why a slim body-frame, a light skin tone or frizzy hair should urge such scathing judgement from my contemporaries, *Blue-eye dolly* and *Blondie* changing to *Berbice Bones* and *Born-in-England*.

These legs that could, in St John Street, prance en pointe on the floor of the sitting room, jump double-dutch or single rope sideways, backwards, spin, skip to any rhyme or rhythm, steer my bike hands-free, balance in hopscotch, swivel the hula hoop; these arms that swung from the tops of the swing, that could throw, spin, grab jacks and ball in one sleight of hand movement; and that 'hot mouth' that 'had a plaster for every sore'...All these counted for nothing, with the gaze of these Georgetown girls falling on the frizz in the front of my hair. All of a sudden any limited ability I had to aim, catch, or guide a ball of any size, from marble to netball, with or without the use of racquet, bat or hockey stick became nil. Any verbal dexterity rebounded back in my throat.

A slow realisation of my inability to understand the wide range of subjects I was supposed to learn, from Biology to Geometry, together with a growing gaucheness in the company of more articulate, sophisticated and sports-minded others, plus the disturbing disorientation that resulted simply from moving from one place to another, would have a cumulative effect I hadn't expected.

I had no 'home' to invite friends to, no friends to cycle with, no parent to pick me up in a car, no knowledge or access to clubs or swimming pools.

There was no Catholic group of friends where like birds let out of a cage we would fly out of the church door, chatter and congregate on the wide steps in a frenzy of chiffon, taffeta and white feather bandeaus. I had moved from a place where I had history and placement to one in which the geographical, spiritual, emotional and social landscapes were completely alien to me.

Shame. And knowing that Daddy too felt shame. A Reynolds Metals Company Scholarship shame. A Berbice girl coming back from Georgetown's posh school shame.

I could imagine any of Daddy's compatriots slapping his shoulders and saying:

"Well Jimbo boy, how is the Scholarship girl doing? We gon give these Indians a run for their money eh? Think we can't be doctors and lawyers too?" And I recalled his consternation that day a year before when the Eleven Plus results came out and were in the newspaper the same time as Tita's death announcement, and Mr Blest from Reynolds himself coming up our front steps to congratulate Daddy on my passing. And Daddy had accepted his good wishes and commiserations, the one balancing the other, and only when Mr Blest had gone did he realise Bruce Blest had passed too and he railed at me and Mummy...

"Why y'all dint tell me the man son pass too?! The man must be think I'm an unmannerly ignorant jackass!"

Daddy straightaway jumped into the pickup and roared away up to Princess Elizabeth Avenue to offer his apologies and congratulations. Then came news of the scholarship, prestigious news: only two or three a year were offered to the children of Reynolds employees, and I, Margaret Harris was one of them.

Angela's prophecy that I, this grand-daughter, would 'walk', born of my breech birth, my almost-fatal fall out the window, and my journey to the market at three, was even more firmly cemented with the news of the scholarship. This child's journey had begun. Here I was crossing water already, at the tender age of eleven.

The scholarship girl was caught up in a whirlwind. The *Berbice Times* came to take my picture. We journeyed to Georgetown to visit the school, to buy books and uniforms, seek accommodation. Years later I found out that a Corentyne boy, seeing my picture in the paper, wrote me a love letter, asking to be pen friends; no-one told me, not Mummy, not Ruby, and certainly not Daddy. Miffed? I was more than miffed! They hadn't even kept the letter for me.

In Georgetown, nobody, it seemed, was able to have this country girl. None of those uncles or aunts with their big houses and their Georgetown jobs. The clerks and office girls had developed with the country into managers and accountants, personal secretaries and telephonists. They had homes to run, their own children to ferry to and from school. In the future I would wonder how much this decision affected the course of my year at St Rose's. At the time, my mother tried to gloss it over, saying it was because of this, or because of that. Some obviously felt they didn't want the responsibility of someone else's child but although as an adult I have witnessed the effect of other people's children on even the most generous and easy-going of households, there still remains the feeling of being let down. For many Guyanese families, hosting the children of relatives while they studied was of primary importance. The Caribbean has a history of families 'taking in' relatives for one reason or another. The Williamsburg brood itself was direct evidence. Aspiration was everyone's goal. Education was at the fore; family children were sent to share bedrooms, a desk found, and the new member to the family contributed in any shape or form, be it financial, or at least an extra pair of hands. But Indians knew who they were; knew where they came from; placed their Gods and family unity right up there at the top.

Our mixed race family had no ancestry that they acknowledged being proud of (apart from the White Barbadian), no common religion or culture; we came from a background of displacement, from diverse and unremembered geographical locations, broken tribal and opposing platforms of power; we were a mismatch of cultural and social climbers, distancing ourselves from the plantation with every step we took.

Georgetown was the buzz, no doubt. Swimming, tennis, ballet, parties, drive-ins. Country cousins who'd just graduated from using a spoon to a knife and fork, who couldn't swim or play music, run fast or buy readymade clothes from Fogarty's, had never flown in an aeroplane, or couldn't boast Abroad holidays, belonged where they came from: the bush. Georgetown was grown-up, its people slick and fast-talking. Couples kissed openly along the seawall, no shame.

"Hold your handbag close, this isn't Berbice," Aunty Somebody says, taking the country cousin along Water Street past Bettencourt's Store where cheap watches and hula hoops, pen and pencil sets, playing cards, plastic bandeaus and hair grips glittered from the pavement. The pedlars shouted louder than they did in New Amsterdam: you needed *this* penknife, *these* batteries. Stabroek Market could swallow its New Amsterdam sister whole. So could St George's Cathedral, *the largest wooden building in the world, girl.* Young ladies swung their stocking-clad feet off the high stools in Booker's cafeteria, and the boys lounged with sunglasses down their noses. Georgetown houses even smelt different. The radiograms were more modern, the furniture more streamlined. Your cousin's hairbrush seemed to possess a different quality, the Cutex bottles a wider range of colours.

But even as you watch those big ships move down the Demerara or check those cool clothes from Toronto hanging in Fogarty's with prices that could pay the light bill for a quarter, you're learning there's another Georgetown.

You hear it in the adults' conversation: *I don't know what this country is coming to*; in their reaction to the news, in open and heated debate about what kind of country it will be with the British gone. There is a Georgetown with Choke And Rob men, and Watchmen, and iron grilles at the windows and doors, and mad angry dogs chained up in the smallest of yards. Some were even Alsatians, a newly popular breed who needed special food, walks, and training. The dog alone was a hundred dollars and that didn't include the chain.

Another Georgetown, of trade union disputes and riots, political parties voting on the basis of colour, of looting and burning buildings some of whose inhabitants were still inside, like that entire Abrahams' family whose photographs covered the whole front page of *The Sunday Chronicle* in 1964. Dawning awareness came to me through the radio, that smartass brown-polish Phillips thing that offered pop music and stories, funeral announcements and bad news. I remember that time it seemed the whole of Georgetown was burning, store after store catching fire and hourly the radio filling us in. *The mob are now rushing towards Lamaha Street, incendiary devices were seen to be thrown at the cinema...*My mother and father circled round, ears opening wide as the conch sprawled on the doily.

There was a Georgetown of poverty; not only what you could see, like the beggars by the bus stops or the women at Bourda Market selling half a dozen limes and two mangoes, sitting on a torn sugar sack with a dry-eyed baby seeking the shade behind her mother's back, no: hidden poverty which I only saw that Christmas when our group of St Rose's girls in our crisp uniforms visited the housing scheme to hand out hampers, and from the slit behind one door where children burst out like vines in a profusion of self-conscious smiles, a silent, expressionless black woman stood inside the gloom.

How different up at Ruimveldt private estate, where Booker's looked after their top workers, settling them in behind security gates, in sprawling concrete houses with a tennis court in the grounds. Their exquisite children glided home in chauffeured cars, pausing at the gate where the security guard would nod and raise the barrier. Leather shoes galloping up the concrete steps, rushing across the polished floor, past the telephone gleaming from the mahogany table, headed for bedrooms boasting record players and Polaroid cameras. There would be no pictures of Jesus Knocking at the Door here, or magazine cut-outs of the Royal Family. Instead, a silver replica of the Eiffel Tower or a print of Manhattan at night.

A place had been found for me to stay with my mother's good friend Sharon. They used to go to the cinema in New Amsterdam nearly every week, entering a world of handsome leading men and beautiful starlets, romantic trysts and happy endings. Cary Grant, Clark Gable, Lauren Bacall...I guess they would have blinked, just as I used to, coming out the Globe Cinema, stepping out of Monte Carlo into the path of a donkey cart piled high with water coconuts.

They'd have gone dancing Saturday nights at CMC, my father dressed up to the nines in smart suit and black patent leather shoes with spats, my mother and Sharon in pink or tangerine brocade dresses with matching high heel shoes...Then Sharon had met and married Harry, a Corentyne boy, and together they'd moved to Georgetown where they now had a baby daughter, Annette. They lived in a downstairs apartment in a yard off Main Street, just ten minutes walk from St Rose's.

I come back for lunch, along the avenue beneath the

Emperor palms. I enter the gate of the yard to the sound of Sharon singing to the baby. Annette is pretty with dark hair as straight as a die; probably got that from Harry, as Sharon is what they call dougla, a mixture of Black and Indian, and her father is half Chinese. I can smell curry bubbling away on the stove and my belly rumbles. Sharon looks tired; she passes the baby over and wipes her forehead with the back of her arm.

"O Lord, is one o'clock already? Food an done cook yet!"

My spirits sank.

This wasn't the first time. I was starving; it was a long time since breakfast, bread and tea, and all the commotion with Harry yelling he didn't have a clean shirt and the baby keeping them up all night. Yesterday I had been given a cup of corn for lunch.

"Have a cup of corn and some bread," Sharon says now.

"You can have double helpings of curry and rice this afternoon."

All afternoon in class my belly rumbles; I keep clearing my throat so nobody would hear. For years and years I wouldn't be able to eat corn.

And in the world of school, Mother Superior sails, a sleek dark ship amongst her Ursulines. These are the torchbearers of the Mercy Sisters, who came to British Guiana a century ago, a pioneering band of women with torches blazing in their hearts. These are the women who had taken in my aunts Ismay and Sybil after their mother Palmyra died, teaching them secretarial and dressmaking skills before turning them out into the world. St Ursula smiles benignly down from the wall. Ask my Aunt Ismay now about that time and she will tell you she can't remember a thing.

Mother Superior comes to rest in front of me. On the other side of this solid wall Camp and Main Streets hurtle past. St Ursula's smile is reflected in Mother Superior's, as a thumb caresses my forearm, smoothing the sleeve of my white blouse into what should be a precise, pencil-sharp fold $x$ inches above my elbow. Back in New Amsterdam, my illustrated prayer book depicting the saints and all their sufferings: the whippings and burnings, the scaldings and deaths by arrow, by burning oil, by gouging: bore smiles such as these on beautiful, exquisite faces. It hadn't been long since I had practiced that look of shining grace in the bathroom mirror, towel clenched tight around my oval face.

When Sister goes out the classroom, some of the girls turn to me.
"You don't miss your Mum and Dad?"
"Which church do you go to?"
"How come your eyes blue? Portuguese don't have blue eyes."
"I have a Scottish grandfather."
"You wha...?"
"We an believe you. You does go there?"
"Which part of Scotland?"
"You lie!"
"No!"
I have begun to feel I've wandered into Wonderland, I am shrinking under the gaze of the Red Queen. The lie pops out so easy.
"I was born there."
"Born where? Scotland?"
"No, England."
Once out, the lie started to live a life of its own.
"You lie!"
"Why should I lie? I can show you a picture if you like." Elizabeth had plenty of pen friends all over the world, including England, like that Mrs Butler with her four boys who she would joke she would marry her four girls to. There was bound to be a picture of a baby in a pram somewhere.
"How come you don't talk with a English accent then? You sound just like Guianese."
"I am Guianese! I mean...I was just a baby when I left!"
"So you was a baby in England? How old were you?"
Alice in Wonderland was now in the dock. I was in her pocket.
"Three."
"Three? Huh. You lie. What you remember then?"
"Not much, a pram, a park..."

"You really lying fuh true! Nobody can remember from that small!"

"Yes I can!" I snapped. "I even ..." I bit my lip. Why did I lie? How could I tell them I could remember from age two and a half? They bound to catch me out then. Luckily Sister came back, and everybody shut up promptly and bent their heads back down to their books.

But they didn't let up. Now they had something to get their teeth into they worried it and worried it. I had created a huge bone for them to gnaw on. At break times in small groups they would come up and ask me again and again if it was true I was born in England and if it was true it was cold bad even in summer and what milk my mother feed me on and did my Scottish relations ever come to visit and did I visit and who my daddy was.

The watercolour of myself began to run. From anonymity I had become the class joke with 'Born in England' stamped on my forehead. And then one morning my tongue grew fat in my throat and refused to uncurl. B...b...born in England. Physics and Maths were hieroglyphics swimming on the blackboard. Most of the time I'd be made to stand facing the blackboard, unable to answer, or for giggling with Melissa at the next desk. Melissa was an a class joke too, because she was fat; but being American, she was not quite as unacceptable as a lying, half-white-no-folks Berbice girl.

But whilst the words lodged in my throat, they spilled out on paper. Book, my friend from days of old, came bounding in disguise. No more war comics from Christopher, or Fred and Wilma Flintstone, or even Mummy's *Woman's Own* magazine. Book came disguised as something called Literature; but he was still Book taking me to Dreamland, where retorts and quips came to life with question marks and exclamation marks, and possibility trembled at the turn of every page. My pens and pencils led me, just as the needle did, spidering into imaginary worlds.

The brother and sister in the apartment next door to Sharon were always out playing on the concrete. They were younger than me and still in primary school, but loneliness after school drew me to them. We would play jacks, and marbles, and I would temporarily forget I was seventy miles away from home and my sisters, from skipping in the street or bush-cooking with Loretta.

I was so grateful for their friendship I took up the boy's dare to steal Harry's razor blades from the bathroom cabinet.

I had already helped myself to one, and had shaved away the frizzy bits of my hairline which I had got conscious of, the way the girls stared. Harry hadn't missed that one but he missed these.

All hell broke loose.

"You got thief in the house now!" Harry accused Sharon. "That's what come of taking in other people's children!"

But even before that, there had been trouble. He was always out. There were rows. The full time care of Annette flustered Sharon. The ironing piled up. She argued with Harry every night when he came home late from work, and where was he going at weekends without her? Then she began talking to herself, turning her head to an imaginary voice: *yes I listening*. She was speaking to no-one in particular; and that's when another place had to be found for me.

As before, no relatives put their hands up. There had been the odd invitation, a trip to the drive-in cinema once, an overnight stay. But no more than that. Who's to blame them? I can just hear someone saying *See?! I tell you Family is trouble!*

Friends of friends were eventually found, 'Aunt Lily' and 'Uncle Fred' with their two teenagers, Brenda and Samuel. They lived in Bourda, just around the corner from the market, amongst a hub of shops and residential houses. Apart from his obsession with dissecting frogs and chasing me round the house with his victims, Samuel was fairly easy to live with. He attended Queen's College and had aspirations of being a doctor.

Brenda was something else. Any hope that she would be a chummy big sister taking me liming round Booker's to try on clothes or perch on the stools at Brown Betty's on a Saturday was instantly zapped. She had disliked me even before she met me because she was being made to share her room. There was also an age gap of three years between us which, for a teenager, is unbridgeable. She was a school rival, a Bishop's High School pupil: *St Rose's girls are stuck up Catholic snobs*. Although I didn't know it at the time, there may have been another reason, perhaps two: this white skin of mine did not always do me favours; there may have been some jealousy, some element or memory trace stemming from history where light-skinned people were given preferential treatment by being appointed as house slaves and not field Negroes, and thought to be above themselves. Brenda may also simply not have liked me.

Perhaps I was not very likeable. Back home I was thought of as being argumentative. Here I was told I was sulky, although quick to forget a disagreement. Inside I was neither of those things; I simply felt gauche and sorrowful and often hid my inadequacies by playing the part of a clown, but at this particular time perhaps my unhappiness just made me unpleasant to be with.

Whatever the reason, Brenda flounced and snarled and warned me not to dare touch her things, cramp her style, or get in the way when her friends came round. She complained to her mother if I picked up a magazine or moved her nail polish six inches along her dressing table. The conversation between her and her girlfriends would come to a sudden stop if I walked into the room, or passed them on the veranda. My lowest point came one evening when I sneezed at the dining table and Brenda threw her plate of food out of the window into the yard below, saying I had contaminated it.

I write in my diary, July 3rd, 1966:

*Everybody has shunned me today. B is disgracing me before her so-called friends and I am embarrassed. I want to go home.*

I had tried to do all the things I'd been taught: being polite, making my bed, helping with the washing up. I went to church too, sometimes to Brickdam Cathedral, but as the only Catholic in the house I had to go alone, a strange, alienating experience, which made me hide behind the pillars in case any of my classmates saw me, 'Born in England', a Lonesome Ownsome. Back home in New Amsterdam,

Church had been an outgoing social experience, right from the moment you stepped out your door, walked up St John's Street, said good morning to whoever was heading your way, admired Cora's new dress. Sunday after Sunday, the same faces each time, the nodding in the pew, the gathering outside afterwards to chat. Here, I felt like a huge pillar myself, Lot's wife, salt, and wished I could melt away. The thought crossed my mind: did my Daddy ever feel alone in his church? But it wasn't quite the same thing: we might have been up the road at the Church of Ascension, but he was still surrounded by people he knew; he could walk out the Anglican church door with his own little gathering and an escort of townspeople would be greeting him – *Good Morning Captain* – on his way to meet us.

Many instances of loneliness resurface: me calamitous at hockey, on my ownsome on the pitch with only Melissa to talk to; overhearing classmates being invited to parties or the Kingston pool; the laughter on the playing field as I sat on a red ants' nest; the whisper of *Born in England* on the stairs; the incomprehension during lessons, the slow walk in the hot sun back to Bourda wondering what mood Brenda would be in.

And then I made a friend.

Someone who didn't care if I was rubbish at hockey or lawn tennis, came last at running and stammered. Someone by the name of Clare, half Irish, half Indian. Her father was a doctor and they lived in a large house near Lamaha Street. At last I had someone to visit, to walk with, to sit with at lunchtimes; to say on my behalf, *if she says she was born in England, she was born in England*. And walking one day along the avenue in Main Street, the Governor-General's wife stopped to talk to us, admiring our school uniforms, and I remember being chatty and cheerful, and proud to be a St Rose's girl. That one moment I would always remember, a micro-second of belonging to the school, to the city, reinforced by the presence of Clare.

But it was too late.

One evening, putting the dishes away whilst a grudging Brenda washed, I misjudged the positioning of a plate on Aunt Lily's plate rack. In concertina fashion, the plates slid off the rack onto the floor, one following after the other: Aunt Lily's entire dinner service. A brief breathless silence was followed by Aunt Lily's piercing scream, and a look of terrified pleasure on Brenda's face. *I told you so*, her eyebrows said; *I told you so*, her long fingernails repeated, bending down to retrieve whatever survived.

Daddy was called from New Amsterdam. I was the one to open the door to him. He looked like a haunted man, his face *as long as a pot spoon*, to use one of my mother's sayings. He stood there with his hat in his hand, as dark as rain clouds.

As well as annihilating the crockery, I had failed in every subject except Art, English and Needlework.

When Baba's car came to pick us up it was pouring with rain.

1966, and the country girl was going home.


I got a place at Berbice High School. For all its dilapidated appearance, it was noted to be the best high school in Berbice and children travelled from as far as Skeldon to study there. Some even boarded with relatives in New Amsterdam. Most of the teachers had studied abroad and boasted degrees from Massachusetts, Paris and London.

Because I had done so badly at St Rose's I had to do First Form again. That meant that some of my classmates were a year ahead of me. But I didn't care. I wasn't like those elegant girls entering their second year, comfortable with the chemistry lab, the sports field, the auditorium. Not me with my skinny legs and my new stammer.

My voice took its time to appear. The alphabet lurked at the back of my throat for weeks; D, P, and B took the longest time. But nobody had to ask me where I came from.

Dolly from next door cycled with me the first day, showed me where to park my old bike, where my classroom was. Although many of my classmates were from New Amsterdam, several came from the Corentyne, from the sugar estates, and Blairmont...Some were rich and some were poor. Some were the sons and daughters of managers. Some were sugar workers' children, their lunch pails cooked by early rising mothers before the sun was up, and they travelled miles by bus down the Corentyne Highway or across the river.

A pretty Indian girl speaks to me by the bike shed. I don't understand her at first; her first language is Hindi and the English words unfamiliar. But she is just asking me where her classroom is. Me!

At the end of the school day I don't wait for Dolly; I have the wind under my pedals.

The next day I ease my bike into the rack, a bunch of girls from the convent are with me. Then the Indian girl appears, smiling shyly. She speaks to me in her halting English, and my friends laugh.

"You don't want to speak to *her*," one says. A flash of my former self at St Rose's fills me with anger.

"I'll speak to who I darn well like!" I snapped. "What's your name?" I ask, turning to the girl who stands nervously beside me.

"Devi," she whispers.

I grab her arm.

"Come on Devi, you walk with me."


To and from school I cycle along Main or Water Street, white shirt, navy blue bow tie and pleated skirt. Pass those streets I know and begin to know like the back of my hand, pass faces I've been used to seeing all my life. It is not like walking from Bourda to St Rose's, Lonesome Ownsome, but then again I find I miss Georgetown's Main Street, the cut and buzz of the city; miss Clare, miss that sense of being in an important place, that knot in my belly.

This was a feeling that has continued: always wanting to be somewhere else, following academic or artistic opportunity then getting homesick, and when I return home, realising what an opportunity I have had and can't wait to go off again! The idea of home itself has preoccupied me to an extent I would never have imagined.

# 16

# Boys, Boys, Boys

Suddenly there are boys.
Tall boys with brown eyes, green eyes, curly hair, straight.
They hook their bruised legs on the handlebars of their bikes and freewheel down the street. I can do that too, bet Christopher I can stay steady for longer than him. Girl children gather at the gate.
*So-and-so is passing.*
*Is the same boy eh?*
*Is the third time he passing. He must be love some girl down here. I wonder who it is.*
"Hey boy! You got girlfriend don this street?"
We giggle and rush inside the yard.
Rover doesn't need any encouragement to chase anybody riding a bike. His temper's got worse. Being thrown out of the window when you're a puppy is bad enough. Having children ride on your back is par for the course. Losing an eye just because you want to accompany the mistress of the house to the cinema down that busy Water Street is no joke. How is a dog supposed to do his duty with one eye, or on a chain?
He looked mournfully at me. I'd been gone a long long time and now I was back I didn't have time for him, just swung on the front gate laughing at boys. How he wished he could get his teeth on their ankles, or the seat of their pants, like that time he nearly got that bad-breath postman. They kept him on a chain all the time now; life just wasn't fair. *You wait, you wait, time a come. You gon miss me when I gone.*
Grocery boys, schoolboys, altar boys...There's no cuter altar boys on the whole planet. They look like they come straight down from heaven with their pale skin and white gowns. Just like all those Jesus pictures.

Someone had given me a diary and I wrote, on December 16th, 1966:

*Johnny decided he liked me! Well! The children nowadays! He's a nice little boy though. I like him as a brother.*

On the 17th:

*That boy again! Went and showed off in front of me.*

Around this time, Book and me became greater friends than ever. Book slept with me, washed up with me, guided my footsteps up to the Public Library to the Hardy Boys' shelves, the Katy Dids, the Anne of Green Gables. Way at the back of my mind lurked afternoons at St Rose's when English Literature had given me the key to other worlds. But more and more my eyes are straying to the Mills & Boon sections which I am not allowed to take out yet; the sharp eyes of the librarians know who I am and how old I am.

At school I stumble like everyone over long passages of poetry we have to learn: the Scottish ballads, the allusions to cedars from a place called Lebanon, people called Assyrians, news from somewhere called Ghent to somewhere else called Aix. Half of the time I had no idea what they were going on about but had to learn the poems anyway, at risk of being made to stand in front of the class and hold my hand out for a lash of the cane. But what pleased me was the rhythm of the words on my tongue. In some strange way they were marrying up to the consonants still buried in my throat. Together they somehow made music that made me burn to sing out loud.

But this new language of expression was not easy to inscribe. Teenage self-preoccupation fuelled me; temper and frustration ruled each waking moment. My diary bore the brunt of day to day concerns.

*Parents? Hate them!*

I have my miseries, my own Les Misérables...the people in this house ....that dratted old man! Complain:

*...don't want to go to CCD, no matter how Father and BB beg. They teach us trash. I'm sick of learning kids stuff.*

Show off:

*Heaven help me if I'm to choose between JB and Kingsley!*

Despair:

*Today I half decided on committing suicide. The old people, especially <u>him</u> are bloomin pests! Daddy is the horridest man I ever met and Mummy is mad. They all hate me.*
*My darling Fluffy, who was my only love, died – put him out and the dogs ate him. I'll never forgive her, never, never, <u>never</u>.*

There was a world out there, and Book stretched himself to accommodate the new development of his reader becoming a writer. He learnt words like 'fab' and 'mostest', phrases like 'sends me'. He accepted the use of the alias 'Dreamboat', the name I gave to that Indian boy with the Beatle haircut who had begun to cycle behind me on the way to school. The boy would wait on Pitt Street corner with his friend, smile, even whistle, causing my bike to swerve into Elly's, whom I had started to cycle with. Poor Johnny B's name disappeared out of the diary, superseded by Kingsley and 'Dreamboat'. Book sighed as he recorded:

*Thank the Lord I saw Dreamboat today. Two days without seeing him is like lying on my deathbed!*

Elly and I became inseparable, calling for each other each morning, cycling precariously in the head-hot sun, looking at boys, spinning madly out into the traffic so that we fell crashing into the street, bleeding knees and bicycle spokes interlocking. There is nothing Guyanese loved more than an incident. Wedding, crowd gather. Fight in street, crowd gather. Schoolgirls fall down, crowd gather. We slipped out of school once, caught the Skeldon bus to 'give our respects' to someone who had died, and came home hours later to a sound thrashing from our parents.
But all through that year there was talk of Elly leaving; her sister Sally had already left to study in the UK, and Elly

would follow. I remember saying goodbye at my front gate, her in her pigtails with her bike, us promising to write. Later that evening Daddy said:

"So Elly gone eh?" and I burst into tears and ran from the dining table.

It was the first in a long line of goodbyes, as far-sighted parents, looking at the 'way this country is going', sent their children to relatives and schools all over the US, Canada, and England. Family and friends too: Lucille-Anne, Uncle Bert, Aunt Ena, the Rosarios...

But then slowly I began to make other friends, Barbara, Glory, and Lorna. Barbara had long black hair and the prettiest brown eyes I ever saw, shining even though her glasses.

Barbara's father was a photographer and her mother had a hairdressing business; her older daughter Pam had been a beauty queen, Miss Berbice.

Glory's father worked for Wimpey Contractors, active in tarmacking Berbice's pot-holed roads; they had a house near the Gardens. She was open and friendly and threw herself into Guyanese life. You'd see her cycling round New Amsterdam, chatting away to all and sundry, something that sometimes left us with our mouths open. She came along to CCD, our Catholic youth group which held summer schools in Pope Street where we played ping pong, watched film shows and helped Father prepare for the church festivals which seemed to follow one after the other. She was soon coming to call for me, leaning up her bike on the bridge and skipping up the front steps where my mother was charmed by her wide grin and accent as she begged my company on a bike ride.

I had known Lorna since convent school days, but because I had to do Form One again at BHS, she was a year ahead of me. She had the easiest, most laid back nature of anyone else I knew; I can only remember seeing her cross once, and that was over a boy. I was always pleased to see her tall, long-legged figure turn into my street, armed with a book or a magazine she either wanted to lend or return to me. She lived with her parents in Kent Street; her father was a lawyer, and she was the only girl with three brothers.

"You're lucky you've got sisters, girl," she would say to me. "Mummy and me are the only girls in our house. And they want us to wait on them all the time!"

One by one or two or three they would come and plead for me for go out, for a bike ride, to the Graphic Bookstore, to the movies, to a party.

"Please Mrs Harris..."

And these were the arguments that had begun to develop between Elizabeth and me.

Me wanting to puff up my feathers and fly, Elizabeth wanting to pull me back in the nest.

Even Desiree became involved in these battles. Elizabeth called her 'my little Des' in a tone that made me want to reach for the vomit bucket, and when arguments were flying I was the one who was always accused of not listening to my mother.

Mummy had it in her head that I only loved my Daddy, when in fact I was just scared of him. Of course you are not going to answer someone back if you know he will reach for his belt with just one word from you! Mummy's little slaps were nothing compared to a full beating with the cane.

But Little Des was her coat tail, Mummy's girl. There were even times when Barbara came calling for me to go liming (though we called it a bike ride) when, if Mummy and I had had an altercation between us, she would say "Desiree can go but you can stay right here."

In school I thought I was the business, coming second as Cooper House Queen; next time round, Des won it.

And my sister's name would make it into Book, referred to as 'Desiree Devil Dog', which we laugh about now, but at the time led to catfights of the scratching and spitting variety with me throwing her best things out of the window! My little blue diary noted important events:

*The old folk went to the barbecue and dance at CMC. Brought back chicken.*
*They saw Dreamboat and Daddy said his father's a barber. So, who cares? I care for him not his pop! Lionel (yes I have discovered his name) danced with Mummy.*

On the 10th June, 1968, I kissed a boy for the first time. And this is what I would have written if I could be sure Mummy or Daddy wouldn't read it:

*I'm starting to like another good-looking Indian boy. At sixteen, two years older and two years up from me in school, he got his friend to pass me notes and stepped off the path by the Chemistry Lab with such a sweet smile I could have died. So me and BiBi went to Globe Cinema and he and his friend slipped in and sat right next to us! I don't know at all what we were watching but after I write this I'm gonna rip it right up because Daddy read what I wrote about them hating me and lashed me three lashes with the cane saying how can I write such wicked things about my parents and even Mummy shouted how I'm getting too hot for my own good. But anyway Micky...Micky...came in with his pagali friend and soon I could feel his arm dangling over the back of my seat! He smelt of aftershave, like Daddy's Old Spice, and spearmint chewing gum. I could feel his knee touching mine too, and I couldn't breathe. I could hear BiBi crunching away on her popcorn.*
*Even in the dark I could see him look down on my lips and just like a love film he put his head even closer blocking out the screen and our lips were touching! Jeez I could have died what with my heart banging away on my ribs. I was so scared but it was so weird I just couldn't hold back, it was like my lips were an elastic band just stretching to meet his! And besides I started to like the feel of the softness, it was nothing like my fingers when I'd pretended before, the inside even of his lips was soft and smooth, tasting of gum and Coca-Cola. Then my eyes closed all by themselves and I learnt why people do that, it just takes over, it was just like the kisses in the films and in Mummy's Mills & Boons and your mouth just kind of opens and moves about all by itself like it knows...We were like in a cocoon, not Globe Cinema, New Amsterdam. I could just imagine Desiree going Ugh! The thought of her made me pull away; I could just hear her telling me I'm hot and gonna end up bad and it was just as well because the ice-cream girl was starting to walk down the aisle and the lights were going up for the interval.*

On Friday 13th I wrote:

*Tipsy [another kitten] came to us. Found her.*

I had actually brought her home from BHS, where a litter was discovered underneath the Headmaster's office.

I also wrote:

*Went to fête. La di da bad with V. I let him touch me all over and I regretted this later, very much...*

The unwritten lines...

*The VSO's house off Water Street. Man, this was so cool. I didn't need to crash, I actually got an invite! Two of the American teachers are such fun. They're called Gary and Willie Gunboat. Willie is tall with a beard and long blond hair all the way down his back. He wears sandals all the time and cycles round NA on a big old bike. Gary plays the guitar. Fergie was there in a mini shift-dress, looking like a sweetgirl, not our English teacher. She raised her eyebrows when she saw us coming upstairs but I saw GM hand her a beer and she got distracted. She was some sight though when she tried to do the Funky Chicken! Sorry state. Is it true what they say, only we Guyanese have got rhythm? The VSOs were really fêting off, drinking and laughing and playing cool sounds, kidding round with us.*
*"You guys know you're not really old enough to be here!" But I saw GM looking up R's legs. He won't bother checking mine that's for sure.*
*V and JJ were out in the back yard smoking. I have a tough job trying to decide which one of them was the most cute. I was hoping they'd be there, especially V as JJ was taken. He gave me goosebumps just looking at him. I got bold and went down and joined them.*
*"You wanna beer?"*
*JJ passed his bottle over to me for a taste. I sat down on the back step; my legs didn't look so thin when I was sitting. The chain belt I'd borrowed from BB jangled on my hipsters. I*

sipped JJ's beer and swallowed it slow, trying not to make a face.
"You looking pretty tonight Fine Things," JJ said. "Don't you think she looks pretty V?"
He gave V a wink and slid past me on the stairs saying, "Y'all excuse me a minute."
So there was me and V all alone in the yard, with only the light from upstairs barely lighting up the banisters. The music was coming through loud; someone had put on my favourite, Otis Redding, 'Sitting on the Dock of the Bay,' and I started to hum to it. V must have said something I couldn't quite catch because suddenly he was right beside me on the step saying, "He right, you looking real pretty tonight!"
My heart started that hammering thing again. It was only three days since I'd found out what a French kiss was! How did all these boys start to look so cute? Otis was singing about leaving his heart in Georgia and a loud crapaud started up somewhere in the bushes and somewhere above us some girl was giggling away. But these things seemed so far away. I had to make the most of this moment. I couldn't believe one of the cutest boys in NA was spending time with me.
"So how many subjects you taking for GCE?" I asked. His mouth was a hair's breadth away, but I couldn't let him get so close so fast. What would he think of me?
"Don't bother talk 'bout school, man. You like this song?"
"Badbad man."
He breathed in and I felt he was sucking me in too.
His springy black hair was near enough touching my cheek. Someone came down the stairs and he moved closer to me to let them pass.
Whoever it was went into the garage and started clinking about with bottles. V's voice came from somewhere close to my cheek.
"Look like somebody wedging us together," he whispered.
I sprang up, backing against the banister.
"We better go back up," I croaked, sounding just like that stupid old crapaud. "Maybe we can have a dance?"
He stood up too, and leaned back against the other banister, hooking his thumbs into the loop of his jeans.
"We can dance right here," he said, and before I knew it he'd

163

yanked me off the step and pulled me into his arms and started to do a slow grind on the concrete. His hands roved like wild monkeys all over my back; the front of his jeans ground my chain belt into my hip-bone. He slid what I knew deep in my soul were going to be teasing lips down my neck and up my chin and behind my ear with that spearmint tang coming closer and closer to my own mouth. When he did kiss me I was more than ready, though I knew sure as morning JJ would know about this and Gordon and Karl and Latch and all the gang: you know that Harris girl? Well I soor her badbad last night man! But I didn't care. I wanted that kiss, wanted that kiss not only for me but against all those girls who even here threw those names at me: 'bones' and 'skeleton walking'. Here was skinny old me kissing one of the cutest boys in NA. He was holding me so tight. There were girls galore would kill for this. So I let his hands rove, his mouth probe through another smooch number and only when somebody upstairs decided to change the mood and put The Stones on and JJ came bounding down the stairs did we come up for air, both blinking like we were caught in some watchman's torchlight.

November 7th:

End of romance with Micky. To hell with him. He's a real soppy country kid stupid. Ha! Ha! Ha! No man is worthy of me.

Oh Lord. I let XX kiss me. A teacher! He'd tried before, once when I went back in the classroom after school. But that was just a quick thing, a peck. He'd said I look so much like Hayley Mills, so sweet he couldn't resist. But at Cooper House party I saw him watching me. I was wearing my blue peephole dress and so many of my girlfriends were over at Scrimgeour House party I kept flitting between the two and he caught my arm when I was running down the stairs by the Science Lab and he said, "Come in here a minute," and we went into an empty classroom and he sat back on the desk looking at me and smiling. He was only just out of Sixth Form himself, barely four years older than me. Him and M were sweet on all the girls. He modelled himself on the latest Beatle look, long fringe *nearly down to his eyes and curling at the back over his shirt collar. "I think you flirting with me," he said. I didn't know what he meant.*

The word 'extracurricular' was one that rolled easy off my tongue. The interminable length of the average school day was made bearable only by the bits in-between that I was throwing myself into any chance I got. Looking forward to Drama, photography club, choir, a walk across the school grounds with the register...anything to get out of the subjects I hated: Maths, Chemistry, Physics, Geography (apart from the maps). I dreaded taking my school reports home, knowing I would be in for a sermon, a chastisement, a curfew. But I threw myself into volunteering pieces for the school magazine; threw myself into Drama productions, costume design, learning the whole of Hecate's speech for Macbeth.

Excerpt from BHS magazine, 1968/9:

**Dramatic Society Report**
...The greatest praise must be bestowed upon the fourth forms of Berbice High School for their public production, in June, of Shakespeare's *Macbeth* – which was the first time in the history of this school that the Dramatic Society staged a public performance!
Chief in the cast were Daniel DaCosta as Macbeth, Emerita Mohabir as Lady Macbeth, Ian Leach as Macduff, Anthony Burnett as Duncan, Gordon Alphonso as Malcolm, Denholm Kendall as Banquo, Royston Anderson as Ross, Margarette Harris as Hecate, Gail Kyte, Yvonne Blair, and June Ann Thompson as the Three Witches, Romaine Annamanthodo and Pauline Khan as Prologues, Clarissa Mohabir as a Lady, and many others. Invaluable assistance was also given by the students of the lower sixth.

*Hecate, green-toothed and wild-haired, stirring the cauldron on stage drawling that inimitable chant: 'Macbeth, Macbeth, Macbeth' almost loses her concentration as a member of the audience mimics,*

*"Margaret, Margaret, Margaret..." to a roar of laughter from the audience.*

My Drama teacher had cut my long lovely speech to a few lines. It took a while for me to live it down. *Bubble bubble toil and trouble* indeed.

Life was a drama, and Drama was life, I was experiencing it, not only through small moments of engagement, and a recipe of books and films, but with a head full of dreams, mimicry, and a sponge-like memory.

# 17

# Daddy

From nowhere fear implanted itself in my mind.

It had no name. It came as wakefulness in the middle of the night, a rush of vomit to the throat. In the morning I open my eyes hoping against hope that it had gone.

I am alert to the rest of the house rising, sleepy-eyed grumpy children unwilling to dedicate yet another day to school. My mother's voice saying her prayers comes through the walls. A kiskadee calls its sweet namesake. Baby's voice will soon sing its good morning up the back steps.

But all is an illusion. *It* is there still; *it* is running the length of my limbs, the pores of my skin, weighing my head down with a weight I had not carried since St Rose's. Like those entities I have heard about, for which priests and witch-doctors, obeahmen and healers are engaged, coming secretly at dusk, with palms outstretched to receive fair exchange for those services that will jaray, dispossess, cast out, beat out with whips and belts, dark thoughts have possessed me. One minute there I am, mind full of that good-looking boy who sits in front of me at school, who had lent me his ring, walked down the path with me; mind full of the new play the drama group is putting on, what part I will play; mind full of agonising on how to approach my mother about the coming fête, full of the letters I receive from abroad, pen friends from Sweden and England, Vancouver, that letter from the Canadian Embassy justifying the seal culls...but mind not so full it doesn't register exactly when these dark thoughts assume a shape.

I had just finished my homework one evening, there at the desk in the gallery. A car drew up, a horn blew. I looked out. Two men looked up at me through the car windows.

"The Captain there?"

*Commodore*, I mouthed silently. Commodore. Daddy had been given promotion, a day job, a land job based at Everton. I hadn't been all that pleased. No more three-day trips up the river? Coming home every night? Lord, how unfair can You get? I was just about having some success with my mother, sweet-talking her into letting me go to parties...fêtes. *Everyone else is going!* I would plead, reeling off the long list of suitable playmates: the Annamanthodos, the Mohabirs, Barbara, Lorna...and Elizabeth, heart warm still at the thought of young girls and choices, would inevitably relent as long as so-and-so's daughter was going too. But Daddy was a different kettle of fish. *What you want to go party for? You not old enough for those things. You want to be old before your time? You want people to talk about you? You want to start running wild? Over my dead body.*

The men in the car honked again.

"Get the Captain, nuh child!"

My father came out rustling his newspaper. He had started to fret about getting disturbed at home. If anybody came looking for him whilst he was having his meal, they would have to wait out there on the porch till he was finished. All those years of waiting on tides, having to get out of warm beds for midnight or dawn sailings, having to round up crew out of Betty's Bar and organise black coffee for them, were supposed to be done with now he was On Land. But promotion always mean more Responsibilities eh? His face was vexed.

"What happen now?"

"Boys gone on strike Cp'n," was the matter-of-fact answer. "Say they ain going nowhere tonight Boss."

"Damn it all," he said, dropping the paper on the rocking chair.

Commodore shirt on and peaked hat later, he headed for the pick-up.

That was the moment I had sensed the unnamed standing by my side in the gallery. The street was deathly quiet. A few clouds spun fast pass the church steeple. Nobody was shouting at their children. No dogs were barking. No-one was taking an evening stroll. No radios were playing. No crapauds croaked in the yard. There was not a mosquito singing nor a firefly dancing. Elizabeth's sewing machine had stopped too, and she came out and sat in the rocking chair, tuning till she found Radio Demerara. The words *strike* and *looting* came after the jingle. She saw me watching and turned the radio down.

"Will Daddy be all right?"

"Of course. Finish you homework."

She dusted a fleck off the gold Phillips monogram, adjusted the doily, straightened the fat-as-a-fool conch.

The strike blew over, but the rush of cold air that had blown into the gallery that night stayed with me. From nowhere the possibility of Daddy dying had made itself known.

Never once had I imagined my parents' deaths. I'd imagined myself a secret older sister, an older brother, even gone so far as to imagine myself adopted, rightfully belonging to some rich businessman with a big house in Georgetown. I would secretly dispose of my sisters by marrying them all off to the most ugly and loathsome of husbands, with warts, bad teeth and fat bellies. But Mummy or Daddy going?

What did I know about death? A memory returned to me: the last term at convent school, Mrs R's baby...

She had been such a pretty baby: pure white skin, star-apple lips, lying on a cradle of ice. Everyone had been singing hymns, cutting through the smell of Limacol and ginger-lilies, perspiration, the tang of lime.

I remembered with horror the fly teetering at the edge of her dolly-baby lips, some nasty Mister Fly with his Berbice River ways burrowing like wood ants, planting his eggs ready for the soft turned earth at New Amsterdam cemetery...

*You daddy's going to die, you daddy's going to die...*

I dawdled on the way home from school, went to Chu's, ate ice cream as slow as I could, cold choking throats of it. Practiced my lines for the play with renewed fervour. Scribbled the lyrics down for the new Beatles' song as fast as the radio would allow me. Visited Glory and listened to 'Tears of a Clown' over and over.

Lately Mummy had been getting a little vexed with Glory.

"That child don't know it's not polite to come dinner time?"

Glory didn't care about things like that. Even Christmas morning she had come calling, ringing her bicycle bell outside. My mother nearly had a heart attack.

"Tell your friend Guyanese people don't behave like that!"

*You daddy's gonna die...*

Over and over again in my head. Was I going mad? Were these thoughts or voices? I tried not to think of Sharon, her incarceration in the Berbice Madhouse. I tried to pray but the worries wouldn't go away. I didn't even have the nerve to say anything at confession, preferring to invent the sin of being more nasty than usual to my sisters, so that Father would give me such a big penance it would be powerful enough to cleanse my mind. I blamed myself for my thoughts. Weren't we taught *pure thoughts, pure soul? God knows it before you think it...wickedness doesn't come by itself, it has to be invited in.* I couldn't tell anyone either; could just hear them, *Where did you get such thoughts from? You'd better pray for your soul.*

Maybe it *was* my own fault; maybe I did put these thoughts in my head because Daddy was so strict and all I wanted to do was please myself, go out, see movies and boys, look with longing at the trendy jewellery now coming in, coloured beads and large plastic earrings, black and white peace medals on long chains...no way would he would allow me to do any of that, no sirree.

I began to watch him so closely he asked me what I was staring at. I even sat on his lap and teased his black-pepper hair like we used to do, with a ribbon bow and bandeau, making everybody laugh. But I was too big to walk on his back. Mary and Yonnette had that pleasure now.

I tried to take in stuff at school, pay attention in class. Everything was getting harder.

I entered the science lab more willingly when sent to have my nail polish taken off than for my chemistry lesson.

Then one morning my new bike partner, one of the twins waiting whilst I jammed books into my school bag, called me Cat Eye and told me to hurry up. I flew at her, my hands reaching for her throat.

"Don't call me that!" I hissed.

"Have you gone mad?" she spluttered.

"I'm sorry, I'm sorry," I mumbled, appalled. But she galloped off down the stairs, jumped on her bike and took off.

"Margaret, what in The Lord's name has got into you?" Elizabeth shouted. "People just can't talk to you these days. Stop this damn foolishness and get your tail off to school!"

My so-called girlfriend had told everybody. They looked at me with arched eyebrows and open mouths as I came into class. *Madwoman!*

Then on that Wednesday, 9th July, 1969, I woke up with the presence hammering all along my ribcage.

*Daddy.*

It was exam time. This morning was going to be Geography, not one of my best subjects. I could tell you about the capitals of countries, a little about islands and continents. But don't ask me about things like *strata* or *tectonics*. But this was pre-GCE year, and everything counted.

I got up and got ready for school, helping to prepare Daddy's breakfast, my turn.

For some reason I followed him out onto the porch. It was Mary who usually ran downstairs each morning to open the gate for him to drive the pick-up out. Quiet Mary, gentle Mary, the lull between the virago I was told I was, the spoil-chile Des, and the platinum-headed Yonnette who tore around like a puppy.

Halfway down the steps my father stopped and turned to face me.

"You got an exam this morning?"

I nodded. The entity did not allow words.

"What subject?"

"Geography."

He looked right at me, as if he had something he wanted to say, then just said, "Well, work hard."

He turned and continued climbing down the steps, his white hat and uniform gleaming in the bright morning sun.

I went to school and sat at my desk; limped through the questions, stared out of the window and waited. Mr Barran was invigilating.

At about eleven o'clock there was a knock at the door and someone came in and whispered something. I watched as their heads turned towards me. My pen dropped on my desk. Mr Barran beckoned me over.

"Miss Harris, you've been called home. Your father isn't well."

"Is he dead? Is my daddy dead?" The panic, now words had brought the inside out, named the unnameable, was unimaginably worse than what I had been carrying around all these long weeks.

They looked at each other anxiously.

"No, no. He'll be all right. Just get yourself home."

I walked out of the classroom, along the concrete path to the bike shed; unlocked my bike, mounted it, cycled down past the starer's house, the Botanical Gardens, the Nazarene Church. Close to the pavement whilst buses and lorries, motorbikes and cars coughed diesel fumes around me.

The voice, free at last, grew louder in my ear: *I told you so, told you so.*

Then another, *Shut up! Don't be silly, he's okay, they said he just wasn't well, that's all, not well. Teachers don't lie.*

Then, *Please God let this not be happening. Please let my daddy be all right. Don't let him die, please God, please.*

A cycle swerved across Main Street by Ramlall's hospital. Donna..What was she doing out of school?

She cycled alongside me.

"Margaret, oh God Margaret I just heard. I'm so sorry."

"Heard? Heard what? He's going to be okay they said."

"O Lord, I'm so sorry. He's dead. I've just come from your house. I'm so sorry."

"You're lying!" I shouted. "Lying!"

How could Donna do this to me? She was my god-sister for Chrissake. Her daddy born me, for Chrissake, slap my bottom to wake me up into the world. She can't come now telling me my Daddy dead. I sped away from her, my bike weaving in front of an approaching truck. *If I rode my bike towards that truck I wouldn't have to know anything. It can all be just a nightmare.*

But as soon as I turned into my street I knew.

A crowd had gathered at the gate.

New Amsterdam just love Things Happening.

Fall off you bike. Crowd gather.

Wedding. Crowd gather.
Fight. Crowd gather.
Dead house. Crowd gather.

I had to push my bike through the crowd on the bridge. Heads turned. *Ow mih God, is Mr Harris daughter. Poor chile. Poor fatherless chile.* Through a sea of faces, neighbours, shopkeepers, the postman. *I hope Rover did bite you hard, sink his teeth right in you jackass bottom.* I leaned my bike up by the swing. The new dog Rio was running all the corners of the yard his chain would allow, barking to hell and go. He'd never seen so many people at his front gap in all his short life. I made my way up the front steps. Yonnette was in her convent school uniform with some of her school friends on the porch. That same porch just three hours ago I had stood saying goodbye, or not saying goodbye, to my daddy. Three hours and a lifetime, a death time, a nightmare time, a Lord Jesus this isn't really happening time.

Elizabeth was running from room to room, her face white.

"Oh Margaret girl, oh Margaret girl…"

Someone took her arm and made her sit down. The house was full of people. My eyes swung to the bedroom door. Was that where…? People were coming through the front door all the time, talking over and over. Over and over the same thing:

*Oh My Sweet Jesus Mrs Harris, I just heard the news. So sorry so sorry what a shock, but how come, what happen? The Captain only walk past me Tuesday looking a well man, courteous as usual, asking after de family. What strike him down so sudden? The man wasn't sick.*

*He went to work good-good this morning, they bring him home mid-morning, had a bad headache he said, went and sat in the toilet at work then say he had to come home. I make him lie down on the bed call the doctor, doctor come. Oh Jesus what I gon do?!…We waiting for ambulance then Doctor said Elizabeth I'm real sorry you have to say your goodbyes I don't think we can do anything, and my poor Jim just lying on the bed there looking at me can't speak. The man wasn't sick. He went to work good-good this morning. Only two weeks ago he went down to town to have cataracts out of his eyes…*

"Go in and see you fadda, girl."

The bedroom door loomed like a chasm, a stairwell into an abyss. The entity licked itself like a cat on my shoulder. Only half my eye looked at the shape of my father on the bed. The other half looked at the familiar walls, the dressing table, his aftershave lotion. Des was a ghost behind me. I backed out into the hall. Yonnette had brought two of the neighbours' children in, was bringing them in to see Daddy. I went wild; shouted at her, at them, chased them down the front steps.

Faces surrounded me like sheets on the washing line. There was nowhere to hide. I headed for my gallery bedroom and shut the door.

Waking up. I'm hearing some drunk woman sing some hymn that changes from *Way Down the Swanee River* to *Michael Row the Boat Ashore* and she coughing and spluttering and asking for a light and the words *poor fatherless children* crawls under my bedroom door. And the bed rocks and the room rolls just like that time of the earthquake.

Daddy J and Mother had come in on the last boat and DJ took Mummy in the kitchen and said, "Well Elo you free now, you never want to marry the Captain anyway."

And I hear how now my Daddy has gone to his rest at last, Mummy can receive Holy Communion. Because all the time she was married to my Daddy the Roman Church never believe he was a widower. His first wife Adrienne, another motherless Portuguese young woman, had gone mad and walked into the Berbice Bush. No Body, No Evidence. The forward thinking English Church, though, that early font of liberalism which allowed mistresses to become wives and Queens, only needed seven years to certify death through absence.

But not so the Most Holy and Apostolic. No amount of begging will sway a Catholic Bishop.

And now Father D come calling, stretching out his holy hand and say, "Elizabeth my child, now you can be granted the Holy Sacrament."

But my mother find a bumptiousness and answer back a priest and say, "You can keep your Holy Sacrament! Seventeen years I do without it, seventeen years you say I living in sin. I can go another seventeen years without it! Amen."

# 18

# Hot Lime

You daddy dead now, so you can lime. You can run wild, bring all the fire and brimstone down, Lawd. Old James pepperpot mouth can't reach you from Kwakwani, no matter how he tongue ride the current. You mother distress is in the palm of her hand where the Bible don't fill. One month after the Captain dead you want go fête never mind you still wearing black armband. Whilst you momma and sistuh go up Everton to stand amongst those tin-hat, red-face, armpit-sweats paying homage to yuh daddy, as his Potagee wife swing the champagne bottle against the hull of the new *Captain Harris*, boys drool on your front porch. So your momma sends you to Georgetown *change your thoughts* go fêting in Agricola, dance at the Village Gate, stroll the Botanic Gardens with Hazel, cruise Diamond Estate on the back of some boy's motorbike. *Diamond Estate?* Is not that estate Grandaddy Cyril and then Brian James done wuk? Yuh care? Yuh know? Figure that white man and that black man watching you from both sides of the grave! But this is a different world, eh? Hit Brown Betty Ice Cream Parlour where the lightskin and the rightskin swing on bar stools; head for the Rendezvous, check out Hazel's bro Joey and his band practicing in a garage. Spend a day with the rich relations (the ones who didn't want you back in '65, remember?) Then back to the city, drink Kool-Aid at the table with the doilies and the barred Georgetown windows. And there's more: Starlight Drive-in Cinema. Why not? *Change your thoughts.* That black armband thing was just for a month, for show eh? You daddy dead now, so you can stray. All round New Amsterdam, with this friend or that friend, little sister on the carrier. There's no pickup truck cruising looking for his badass daughter. No more wild cane gon whup you ass. You poor mother still distraught, hands full now taking care of the houses, four girl children, light bill, water bill. Relatives rushing in, *Oh Lord Liz, poor Jimbo didn't have insurance, best I run quick get some.* The day after he died one of his brothers dropped by, asked for his glasses.

Just two months after Daddy died Mummy's appendix flared up, nearly killing her. She was rushed into Ramlall Hospital where her Ball O' Fire daughter, me, brought a gang of friends, mostly boys, to see her. My diary entries do me no favours: during that week I took advantage of her absence, went to the cinema; to a fête; dropped off Yonnette to Aunty Jean, and brought one of the boys back to the house where we drank wine and kissed a little! I believed myself in love for three whole days, after which I wrote, *I don't love J. I love life and everybody.*

I went back to school in September in a daze. The children were respectful around me, but I felt a freak. They felt so sorry for me they voted me in as Form Rep. Things were different in other aspects too. Our Headmaster Mr. Beharry, of the impeccable if strictly disciplinarian reputation, had retired and we had a new Head, Mr Armstrong.

I threw myself into every artistic or dramatic activity. In the school magazine Father Britto wrote, 'Miss Margarette Harris was an imaginative costume designer.' Poetry, as well as drawings, began to fall off the tip of my pencil. This too, made the school magazine that year: *Guyana, my country, my love*:

When I wake in the morning and look out through the window,
The wild breeze enfolds me like a warm embrace,
The birds are singing and the palm trees swaying;
"Good-morning" says my neighbour to me.
And although it was the same yesterday and will be the same tomorrow,
I know that nowhere else has the morning breeze,
Nowhere else these gay, singing birds,
Nowhere else these swaying palm trees,

No people can match with ours,
In Guyana, my country, my love.

Sports Day now, that was party time.

We entered the Mad House grounds like the Romans, laughing at the no-teeth old man rubbing his crotch. Cast bold glances up at the barred windows where faces pressed close and arms waved downwards and a young voice wailed *tell me mummy to come and fetch me please*? My stomach lurched and I walked past as quick as I could, not daring to dwell on Sharon, because that's what happened to Sharon after she'd begun to hear the voices. She still heard them, though she'd had all the treatments, even electric shock treatment; and now only her shell rocked on her mother's front porch those times she got let out and Elizabeth climbed the front steps in Trinity St to see her old matinée-going girlfriend, never knowing what to take for her, a *Woman's Own* magazine, or a lipstick, or a cake of sweet soap.

The one thing I did not enjoy on Sports Day was sports. As time went on I grew adept at discreetly referring to periods, feigning sore throats and twisted ankles. I was so bad at everything anyway that the games teacher, especially if it was a man, resignedly gave me ribbons to cut up, or a score sheet to mark. My house, Cooper House, didn't need me holding them up in the relay or anything else, especially with Pugsley and Mackay Houses boasting they were the best. I might have got my voice back through Book, drama and friends, but St Rose's had kept my legs, and hating them the way I did, never mind I rolled up the waistband of my school skirt like everyone else, and grew adept with paper patterns, scissors, needle and thread, to make passable versions of Mary Quant's minis, I still felt that St Rose's was welcome to them. No way was I going to gallop across a field just to be laughed at.

No; the real entertainment on Sports Day was the lime. Two or three girlfriends and you, tie off, shirt collar open, or posing in T-shirt and games shorts, undulating between events in a manner my daddy would have caned my backside for; between the vision of boys whose attention was split between the competition on the field and the parade of peahens sucking on rapidly melting ice poles, adjusting sunglasses, guiding their reckless eyeballs like missiles meaning *shit man you think I staring at you?!* With cut eyes sharper than the sun, preserving their reputations, concealing the hothouse rush of hormonal blood.

Between the girls, the confrontation was full-on: eyeing each other up, checking out the sluts and the bores, rebelliousness making its presence known through the remnants of our school uniform, loose ties, shirt buttons undone, bangles from wrist to elbow, kohl-rimmed eyes, mascara, long Cutex-painted talons, sockless shoes and chain belts accentuating hand-span waists...Away from Miss Thomas' eyes we ran riot. Thin-strapped lace bras zinging. Pale pink and coral lipstick gleaming. Cuban heels. Handsome new teachers, themselves all hormones, Beatle haircuts and assertiveness, eyed us up and chastised us in turn. *Miss Harris, I suggest you make haste to the toilet block right now and adjust your skirt. Ah Miss Harris, how long and dark your eyelashes look today! Miss Harris, you look like a gypsy with those gold earrings!*

I escape with Grace, another sports-shy bookworm, and walk the edge of the Madhouse grounds; pick pods of cotton growing wild in the bushes. All along the Canje Creek lie remnants and ghosts of plantations. That's where the rebel leader Cuffy started his revolt. The Canje River runs into the Berbice; together they head for the Atlantic. Cuffy would be proud: at Independence he took the place of Queen Victoria's stern image in the Botanical Gardens. It had been a long journey for him, from Africa to Canje to Fort Nassau to New Amsterdam Botanical Gardens: two hundred and three years. Wonder what he would have thought of this whiteskin and this blackskin girl playing around with cotton, speaking of Literature.

Two new boys came into our life. By 'our' I mean Des and mine. Yes, me and my stuck-up younger sister had started to lime together. Firstly, KC, a photographer's son, who I had a crush on; and Marix, an Indian boy who became our very good friend. Armed with his daddy's camera, KC took us to the gardens and took photos. I was in my element, posing and sultry, lips ice cream pink with the lipstick my daddy would never have let me leave the house wearing. The Botanical Gardens watched us as we posed. KC positioned us by our bikes beneath palm trees; took pictures of himself and Marix looking mean and moody. When the prints come out we're disappointed how blurred us girls looked whilst the boys' sharp profiles etch into the landscape. *Then* I get the hots for a teacher. A teacher! That VSO Willie Gunboat with the ponytail and the sandals. Rode his bicycle round the town friendly to everyone as those Americans were. Rode up my street, sat on my front porch, charmed my mummy. Life was looking up; I was cool, adult, the business. 'This is a mad time, a time when I do not write between the lines, do not face the turmoil of losing my father. Although people do not stop talking about him, indeed they talk ceaselessly, I cannot remember anyone talking to us children about our feelings.

I can't remember who noticed it first, the smell of the lilies. Those are the flowers that well-wishers had brought into the house at the time of his death. There is a reason why funeral announcements on the radio will sometimes say, *You are requested not to send flowers.* There was another smell too, the smell of perfume sprinkled on the bier as my father's body had lain overnight. These smells returned; highly distinguishable. Strong and pungent in the evenings, in the corner of the dining room, the kitchen.

*He is still here with us.*

Then the destruction started; we would go out and on our return the glass cabinet would be open, a glass smashed. *He wasn't ready to go. He doesn't know he's dead. He's watching out for us.*

Why are we afraid? This is our Daddy.

But we are.

Daddy is a jumbie.

The younger children are crying.

We run out of the house.

* * * * *

The premonition and consequent reality of Daddy's death split my personality totally. In my mind fear leaped like a dog. My precognitive ability left me with constant anxiety that I could not voice. I was living in a house of spirits. *I* was a house of spirits. Spirits lived within me.

My mother has this phrase which is her guiding light: *If your mind tells you not to do something, don't do it.* A variation of it is, *Follow your mind*. This principle is God's guidance for my mother; for those of different beliefs it is a practical approach to life, which unites the body and spirit, cosmic consciousness and common sense. For a teenage girl brought up to believe the unseen, and finding the variegation of Truth, it is an enormous burden. So you wake up on a school morning and don't want to go to school, does that mean something bad is going to happen? Is it not safer to stay in bed; after all, you were warned your daddy was going to die weren't you? Why didn't you tell somebody, Mystic Girl? You could have warned him not to go to work that morning instead of standing on that front step like a dumb fool...If he had stayed home, even if he had still had the brain haemorrhage, the doctor would have got to him in time, he would have been nearer to the hospital, wouldn't have had to travel all the way from Everton slowly dying.

I preferred not to talk about Daddy, hardly mentioned him even to Book, to whom I told everything else.


So much had happened in November alone! There was that nasty-minded man, guess who! Earnest churchgoer and husband to the pale-skinned starer by BHS! Cruised his little white car by the gardens whilst I was riding my bike and asked if I wanted to come for a little drive up the Corentyne! No wonder his poor wife stared at schoolgirls! I put my skids on, but didn't bother my mother with the matter; she had enough to worry about.

I completely failed my half-term exams. This time though, adults made allowances, just like the students who'd made me form rep. Poor fatherless child. I was no longer scared to go home with a rubbish report. The worst had already happened. Elizabeth was not the same, was not up to sitting at the dining table with me as she had at the time of the eleven-plus, with her blend of prayer and a ruler. Even she could not make head nor tail of algebra and geometry. She paid for extra lessons for me with one of the young teachers, Navin Chandrapaul, but I didn't learn a thing. Others did; maybe I decided I didn't want to; preferred to stare across over the bottom-house wishing the time away.

My state of mind and immersion in 'extracurricular activities' might have had something to do with my lack of academic progress. After all, hadn't our biology teacher, Mr Barran himself, say I had the ability; all I needed was to *apply myself*? Stupid people did not get 80 per cent in English.

But there were so many distractions! Gaffy telling me that for a thin person, I had nice legs. Bruce, and Willie Gunboat, who was openly pursuing me with messages through fellow VSO Gary; we even went to the movies together! And then there was the Berbice Arts Theatre, the New Amsterdam drama group which I had joined. Each week I cycled along Water Street, leaned my bike up by the market, went up the staircase into the Town Hall.

Practice, practice, practice: all those lines to learn, all that excitement about the forthcoming play in which I was the girlfriend to the main character.

I also had a new friend, Katie; she had joined BAT too (I hadn't been allowed to hang around with her when my daddy was alive because her aunty ran the local rumshop).

There were parties…I begged Lorna's mother to let her come…she begged mine to let me go…boys to dance with…JJ, Mara, Marix…there was laughing and liming on the dance floor in well co-ordinated/ borrowed/ hastily-sewed clothes, white plastic earrings and long strings of beads.

There was a school trip to Georgetown, to Bishop's High and St Rose's, where a pinhead-sized Margaret passed me on the stairwell and the girls looked down on her from a great height.

Only the needlework teacher, Sister Anthony, remembered me.

Clare, lovely Clare, had gone, had left for Ireland and sometimes wrote to me of guns and soldiers.

Around me still, classmates were leaving, or planning to. Talk swerved around what country we should apply to: England, Canada?

Aunt Ena came home for Christmas. Up to my eyeballs in my own concerns, I'd barely registered the fact of Aunty's leaving some years before for England, though I'd not forgotten our run-ins.

I remembered her from 1963: with my parents away in Suriname, she had been left in charge of us. Her constant niggling had made me run off and hide in Mummy's empty bed, pulling the mosquito net down around me, pretending to be asleep as Aunty wandered the yard, shouting my name. I had burrowed into the pillow; footsteps up the front steps had been swiftly followed by an arm swishing the net aside and hauling me out. The cane was in Aunt Ena's other hand, and voice and lash went to work together.

"Eyes and pass me! No respect! Think I'm easy like you mother! Come when I call you, you hear!"

*Lash, lash, lash.*

So I wasn't looking forward to seeing her, not now life was taking off.

Going to meet Aunty at the stelling. Elizabeth's been getting the house ready, us girls polishing the floor and furniture. Baby cooking a curry.

"Your Aunty will be ready for some Guyanese food after all that water-water English food."

The curry smell so nice we forget how we'd begged to save the life of the fowl bought at market last week. Seeing Baby pluck its feathers and smelling the fresh carcase in the hot water turned our stomachs, but when garlic and onion and geera and garam masala start to fry, mouth water quick-quick.

She busy making ice cream on the back step too, turning and turning the handle of the ice cream maker under the shade of the dounze tree.

Elizabeth hurrying everybody up, the last thing she want was to have her sister-in-law come back from England and look down her nose at her and say, *Elizabeth, you still haven't learnt to control these children and now that my poor brother Jim God rest his soul has gone to his life everlasting is now more than ever you have to be strict with them before they run wild on your hands.*

We all had to put on our best clothes too because not only were we crossing over to Rosignol but first impressions always count.

Mummy seemed to forget was just Aunty, not the Queen. She had done her beauty routine, make-up and hair with plenty hairspray because of that river breeze playing hell with it, and was wearing an A-line dress and her white Bata slingbacks. She always wore slingbacks, even if they had a heel. Whole shoes always hurt my feet, she said. Only one time I saw her wear whole shoes, that time three years ago at cousin Ruby's wedding in Plaisance. Tangerine brocade they were, matching her dress and hat. She had looked like a Hollywood dream. I had begged and begged her to keep those shoes for me for when I was older, but she said no: *they won't be in fashion then.*

I still think of those shoes as I have watched fashions come in and out over the years, like the waves.

Elizabeth had taken off with her sewing after Aunty had left the country; Mary and Yonnette benefited from the practise of newspaper patterns on the floor, material cut out, white collars, sashes, braiding. You only used the dressmaker for something really fancy, and more and more I was sketching what I wanted myself, making my own requests to Aunty Jean or the dressmaker on the backdam.

Desiree was catching up with me now in the clothes stakes. No longer did Elizabeth match us all up. We, I, had started to protest. Seersucker dresses? No siree. White shoes? Double no siree. Top and pants, mini skirt with hipster belt, double row of long beads? Yes please. As for Mary and Yonnette, you just couldn't keep the children clean for five minutes...

Desiree would eye me up and down. "You wearing that?"

I sucked my teeth, heading for the hall mirror.

"Mind your own, little girl."

"Blue doesn't go with pink." I sucked my teeth again, slow and long. Desiree was disgusting for true-true.

"What would you know, Juvenile? Just stay in the junior division, man."

"Better than being hot and wild like you!"

My hand whipped out and grabbed hers, long nails scratching and drawing blood.

"You just leave me alone you nasty mouth you!"

She opened her mouth wide and screamed, squeezing tiny tears out of Daddy's grey eyes. I leaned over her, in heels that added at least three inches. "You just listen to me, you goody goody spoil chile…"

"Margaret!" Elizabeth marched towards us. Desiree held her arm up to display the scratches. It had a nice colour on it already. Good.

Since Daddy had died, there had been rumours, discussions, ideas about us leaving the country. Aunty had followed our cousin Lucille-Anne to Wiltshire, and my Uncle Albert had been gone long long too.

Sometimes my cousins Cyril and Evelyn came to visit us in the August holidays. Evelyn never wanted to go back to Georgetown; would hang on to my mother's skirts, crying.

It seemed that I had been chosen to be the first to leave. Mummy had the houses to sell, not a quick thing in the political climate, and she and my sisters would follow.

*He went to work good-good that morning…* Elizabeth had seen Daddy coming up the front steps, white Commodore hat gold braid gleaming in broad daylight; she'd been sitting in the rocking chair by the window. She'd run to the door before she remembered. That white hat had gleamed in the Anglican church from the centre of a well of flowers on top of the coffin. I had walked down that darkened aisle, eyes dimmed from the bright sun, and it was the first thing I saw. I'd been glad to sit down in that front seat pew, the *family of the deceased* pew, because my legs had felt hollow. The church organ was playing some forgettable hymn. From the corners of my eyes I had noticed my school friends...Rome, the twins, Lorna; they kept looking at me and I felt shame bad, shame rising up like gutter water every time I looked at that hat; shame that my friends could see me crying.

Daddy was still walking out there. The scent of the lilies was suffocating in the dining room. Mummy thought about asking Father to bless the house. Angela said prayers and sprinkled holy water.

He's still there. The house groans under wellwishers. Again and again they go through the whole story. Bits are added: *Somebody done him something as The Lord's my witness. Went to that Dead House the night before, and somebody put something in his drink, musee Dead Water. I told him not to go, something told me...*

*He went to work good-good that morning...*

Over and over again, the story told to that constant queue coming up our front steps. Over tea or cocoa or lemonade or sorrel or rum that phrase *poor fatherless children* became a refrain.

And my tongue broke free, about the Knowing. My mother stared red-eyed at me, able to believe. My grandmother crossed herself and told me I was blessed. And then another surprise, Desiree's story. My grey-eyed Mummy-apron-string sister had her own story to tell, how Daddy had called her aside just two weeks before and told her that he didn't think he had long with us and that she must look after Mummy. I grew so cold then. Not so much because Daddy had chosen my sister, but more the fact that that Wednesday morning when I had been drawn out on to the porch and he had turned to look at me, *he had known*. He had known, and did that mean that he suspected I did too, and there on that doorstep we had both been attempting to say goodbye?

They'd made us kiss him, me and my sisters, kiss his ice-cold skin as he lay in the coffin on top of ice in the hall. *You'll neva see you daddy again. Kiss him for the last time.* And at New Amsterdam cemetery friends had had to hold Elizabeth back from throwing herself in the grave.

\*   \*   \*   \*   \*

I can't remember who replaced Daddy at work, but in a strange sequence of events three Everton employees, my father being one, all died within a short time of each other.

Memory is like ribbons, the way it can unravel. One of those Everton men, Uncle J, had had a live-in wife, Aunty H. They had lived in a big house in the centre of town. Many a time they climbed our front steps to visit, eat, drink, laugh, talk. Aunty H wanted and wanted a baby. Eventually the babies came, one two, three...but soon Uncle J's eyes started to wander and fell on a young girl whom he married. Aunty H was put out on the street. I passed her frequently on my bike, pushing a big black pram along the streets of New Amsterdam with two young children, whilst another trailed behind her. Guyana did not have welfare. She wandered from relative to relative, and sometimes up our backsteps. But the young wife's sister would be stabbed to death by her husband in the grounds of our school; and Uncle J would drop dead out of the blue, not long after Daddy. Tragedy does not have favourites.

# 19

# Love, Love

Of all the brown skin, black skin, light skin boys; schoolboys, altar boys, teachers, boys with bicycles and motorbikes, boys with their daddy car; boys with knotty hair, greasy hair, brilliantine hair, afro hair, smooth hair, curly hair; one shine skin man stand out, his hair Beatle-style, smoking his cigarette between white smiling teeth. King, they call him. The gossips' mouth ran. Bad boy, coolie boy, more money than sense boy. Expel from school, y'know, and ban from driving.

Through the throng on the pavement by New Amsterdam market he strolls, down Water Street, in and out of the Penguin Hotel, climbs on the back of someone's motorbike, into someone's car.

The crowd melts away whenever you pass, and leaves him standing, bleeding out like a starburst. He don't take no notice of you. But from way back in '68 you catch sight of him and your bicycle wobbles as your eyes can't leave him standing there outside Bacchus Photography Studio. From then on bike rides become compulsory quests.

"Leh we ride past so-and-so," you tell your cycling companion of the hour.

"Leh we pass down Water Street again, get some sea breeze." Slow down pass The Royal Bank of Canada, the new Faaz Cinema, the sawmill; his big white house shining right there, by the river.

If you're lucky you might catch him strolling, in slacks and bright shirts, sleeves pushed up to the elbows. You leave your eyes behind you on the pavement, until one day he notices them, pale blue and gleaming, and sees they belong to some skin and bones Potagee schoolgirl, all of fifteen years old, fast gaining a reputation for fastness. He's amused and laughs, and his friends too, from the seats of their Yamaha bikes where they loll, eighteen and nineteen years old, flanked by some Georgetown girl with smooth hair and breasts. You die of misery and wanting, shame and incomprehension, and don't write anything you can't understand yet, not one word in Book, not till now.

Rain, rain, rain. My mother and I are arguing. Our words are flying out the gallery windows like the dust Baby raises with the pointer broom.

Christmas is over. January has begun the year with a long face which looms into the future.

Elizabeth's rage rises as this teenage daughter uses her tongue as a sword. A simple request to lay the table has erupted into a full-blown row. Words fly out of Elizabeth's own mouth before she even thinks them: *blasted disgrace ...living to save funeral expenses! What does this...child...know of the maelstrom that is her mother's life? Boy, boy, boy. Go out, go out, go out. That's all Margaret's interested in now.* Elizabeth hears herself scream she will send her daughter away, and watches temper turn to tears as this daughter bat and balls between being defensive and affronted.

"I'll never forget these things!" I cry, and head for Book, who remains my confidante:

*...I'm going to make something of this year. I shall bury myself into acting and social activities. Don't know whether to believe in God or not. Given the bird. Put on some groovy grains + all mounted to zero. Came by in F's car. No big thing. But I hurt too much to cry and I'm still mad about him.*

Ocean opened up in the heavens.
Passed him on the way to school.
Rain, rain, rain all the time.
He asked in sign language what's moving.
No big thing.
Rain.

Again and again I relived Old Year's Night, the feel of his mouth on mine, the feel of him as we danced, the feel of his shirt, his chest under my fingers. Everything else was a temporary distraction, a mosquito to be slapped away.

I lost my role as Form Rep to Annie Barran. They only gave it to me in September because they felt sorry for me after Daddy. And anyway, who needs the responsibility?

I visited Aunty Vera's new house in Kent Street, and borrowed the Donovan LP Elly had sent. Some months before he died Daddy had dismantled the playpen in the gallery and had made me a desk, with shelves for my books; I would sit there drawing and looking out through the window in turn. Once he had come up behind me and I felt myself grow hot because what I was drawing was the faces of two people kissing, faces and hair, positioning their mouths. I could hear him sigh behind me, feel his disappointment as he went back to his newspaper.

Now my eyes were permanently peeled at the window just in case *he* passed by. This new thing, *him;* that Old Year's night that still seemed so surreal, so caught up with other things, that moment *he* had spoken to me, that moment I overheard what he said: *that Portuguese girl up there like me bad man*...then the kiss...he had kissed me! *Me!* Him so grown up and all, so *manbody*, so popular, so out of reach of little skinny me. These boys I've been playing around with, they just boys. This is something different.

Out of the blue he walked up my front steps, perched on my front porch; my whole body trembled. After all this time, coming to see me, *me*, not some beautiful Georgetown girl; *me*. Skinny-legged, flat-chested, flat-nosed (despite Elizabeth's efforts), fat-lipped frizzy-haired me.

I thought about him day and night. His face rose up from the pages of my school books. It had been hard enough to concentrate before; now it was impossible. The idea of school began to seem meaningless, what had that got to do with this mad rush of feeling that only he existed in the world?

I began to skip school, drifting about the house with a list of real and imaginary afflictions.

I relived each moment again and again; the smell of him stayed close, the memory of his mouth, the wry smile, the sudden laughter, the stroll of his legs down the stairs, the drop of my heart.

I would sit on the front porch listening to the day die, the birds roosting, the singing of mosquitoes, the croaking of crapauds rising up from the yard. The radio, my comforter, played in the background. I had learnt to know the contours of his face, the brown eyes, the long dark hair in the Beatle cut, the slightly curved nose, the lips, they way they curled ...I couldn't believe they had actually kissed me, at midnight, Old Year's Night, 1969/70.

I still couldn't believe it when he had climbed up our front steps that first time, and my mother had looked at him with her eyebrows raised; but then, she too soon fell for his charm; she knew he was not just one of those puppy-like boys who stood politely at our front door, slicking their hair down after bolting up feverishly. This one walked up the steps as if he owned them, after lifting the bar off the gate as a warning, and of course I got to the door before his arm had even raised for the rap... smoothing my dress down, yet at the same time trying to be 'cool'.

But then I began to know what it is to expect, and what it is to be disappointed.

Big boys have lives that are not shaped by school hours; not by friends asking about homework, borrowing a book, chatting about the latest drama in the classroom or on the sports field, laughing and gossiping and dreaming of a life after exams.

Big boys inhabit a different world, a world of men, and girls, of bars and drinking, free from curfews, able to go out when and where they like. So when a big boy says "I'll drop by tomorrow," he means "I might." And if he is unable to, and makes it the next night instead, she should be pleased, this schoolgirl whom he doesn't know what he's doing with anyway. Her eyes should welcome him surely, not darken at his approach, hurting and trying to wrestle with this new hurt and trying her best not to say "What happened to you last night, then?" in the lightest of tones.

And the porch became a resting place where I would listen to the night die. And the porch became a cathedral where prayers were whispered into the sky. And the porch became a place of glory when his legs walked up the stairs. Would become a battleground of arms and legs and emotional pain.

Then there came the evening to die from, the shame and

ignominy of it. Elizabeth was at the Immigration in Georgetown and Angela was staying with my sisters and me. Came a whistle from the street below, a low rattle at the gate, a cigarette tip glowing in the darkness. My quick steps running downstairs, wry whispers through the gate, his brown eyes careless.

Then the shame.

Later, lying under the mosquito net, I could smell Mother's cigarette from the hall. Imagined it curling up to the ceiling, thinning out in the eaves where the bats were now awake. There were small holes in the net and I was always afraid they would find them while I slept; would crawl through and suck my blood and make me a vampire. There was a whole night-time life that went on while you were sleeping. Mice scuttling along the floorboards, risking mousetraps and the cats, cockroaches waking up in the kitchen, spiders dangling from the bathroom pipe, footsteps on the street outside in yachting shoes they thought no-one could hear, our dog Rio barking, his chain dragging, the ceaseless crickets; Daddy and the lilies wandering round the dining room.

Why there?

The river, black now and silent, with some other captain guiding *The Captain Harris*, that new tug they named after him, which Desiree had watched Mummy try to smash a champagne bottle against. And *him* too now, making plans for his own trip there, for that was what he did, worked his father's sawmill, logged up that very same river Daddy's first wife had disappeared into, and for whose tides Elizabeth had set most of her married life. The memory of my grandmother's words returned as they had dropped down through the gallery window.

"Yuh think yuh coulda hang about allyuh Indian people girlchile gate like that!? Is shoot yuh blasted tail is whuh coolie man would do! You haul yuh tail away right this instant from awee house yuh hear! Come taking advantage of we girlchilren! And Margaret you bring *your* blasted backside upstairs right away now!"

He had laughed dryly, and walked away slowly, and with shame like a bucket of cold water over my skin, I had slouched back upstairs and into bed where hour after hour, between short spurts of sleep, the words repeated and repeated themselves, raw and sharp as onions.

The next morning, for the first time ever, I was glad to see the back of my grandmother as she made to board the launch to Kwakwani.

Gone was the time I was sorry to see her put her going-out dress on, position the Panama hat on her head, pick Polly's cage up and head for the door. Time was when a donkey cart would be waiting to take her and the goods she had bought for the Kwakwani shop to the stelling. And we children would run behind it, try to jump on the back of the cart for a ride to the top of the road. But my father had made his disapproval known: *Tell you mother to order Sawh taxi, I got a position to live up to here.*

I would cling to the talcum powder and Lighthouse cigarette smell of her, thinking of the empty space she would leave. But now all I could think of was the abuse she had given to one of New Amsterdam's top-notch boys. My world was disintegrating; never again would I be able to stroll or cycle the streets of New Amsterdam, never would he speak to me again.

He would tell all his friends and they would laugh and wash their eyes on me each time I passed their gap, the hangouts by the photography store, or Betty's Bar. And my friends, what would they say?

Prayers again, *Dear Lord...*

And the Lord smiled and the Lord listened and who says that prayers are not answered and that there are no miracles, that the sun doesn't shine after rain?

The very next evening he climbed up my front steps with laughter at his heels, repeating with gusto the verbal abuse from my grandmother the night before...*Allyuh coolie people...! Awee girl children...*I myself began to see the funny side, and as ever, not being able to breathe when he said goodnight, bringing his face so close I thought he'd been about to kiss me.

*News* Amsterdam began to live up to its name.

"Margaret's river-man!" they giggled, over ice creams in Chu's, or ice-poles outside the tuck shop.

I glared at the crowd I'd used to move with, sitting with their half white legs and tennis racquets slung over their shoulders.

He played hot and cold on my front porch.

"Let me tell me you something, everywhere I went in this place somebody was always telling me something about you."

*Wild girl.*

In the new year, Book had shape-shifted; the small blue five year diary could no longer contain all that I wished to write. When I cast my eyes over my spidery entries from 1966 that *child* did not seem to be me. This time Book spread himself to become an A5 hardback notebook:

January 24$^{th}$, 1970

*24 days. That's all it took to fall in love. He hasn't kissed me since CMC. Came this evening. Said we can't go on. He loves me very much but I'm going away. If we go on we'll fall more in love + it will be harder. I know it's true but I can't understand. He said he won't be coming back to visit me. I tried to dissuade him, I know he was showing more sense but I don't like reasoning. I prefer my dreams. He said he was never in a position like this.*

January 25$^{th}$

*Woke up with a solution. A foolish solution, we could get married? If I came back next August. I don't know what to ask God for. But I'd like him to come to my party. Told Mum I was gonna marry him. She said his parents would want him to marry an Indian girl.*

The talk of migration had begun to invade our thoughts. The bleeding away of school friends continued. The older boys headed for colleges and universities in the UK, the

States and Canada after big send-offs, pictures in the paper, the lot; others disappeared overnight so discreetly that sometimes I would realise that I hadn't seen Gordon or Frencho lately and someone would say *oh don't you know, they left last week.*

January 29$^{th}$

*I love you, I love you.*

January 30$^{th}$

*...the fête tonight. They were playing jump-ups and I only danced with 2 boys besides him. Then they started playing waltzes and we danced together all the time. It was all so beautiful. His hands moving slowly on my back, his cheek on mine, our lips so close together. He didn't kiss me because everybody was looking at us...I think they saw how much we were in love. Then when we weren't dancing he had his arm round my waist and my head on his shoulders. I know he has respect for me, because the way we were feeling, we could have left the fête and gone...and made love somewhere. But he didn't. When coming home, we were very close together in my street. He turned to me, put both his arms around me + touched his lips to mine. As soon as he did that, we lost control. Our lips were glued together + his hands were holding me tight. God, how I love him! I love him so much it's agony. This love is <u>pain</u>!*

So you're almost sixteen and trying your best to write about passion. Did the Mills & Boons help? All those movies you saw? Beautiful young men and women dressed to the nines, troubled by despair, misinterpretation and distance? You were learning how bad it could be.

How hot you were for him! How roughly you grabbed his hair and clutched the back of his neck like some madwoman. Your mouth was wide open, you wanted to swallow him up. How you loved your lips then, those lips you used to wish were not so full, would stand in front of the mirror pulling in. Now you roamed them over his mouth, lifting your neck to the moonlight like one of Dracula's babes, wanting him to bend you right back and devour you. You in some brief dress that the bones of his hips ground against, pressing against the tops of your thighs towards the very centre of you melting, running like a river in the middle of St John Street in that still pitch black morning just outside your own front gate while upstairs and all around you people were sleeping in their houses with you father not cold in the ground yet and that sawmill son hot-hot underneath God decent sky. Suppose somebody did see you? Somebody getting up to drink a glass of water, smelling passion through the jalousie, catching a slice through the dark window where the moonlight drop right there in the middle of the street whose lamps were all out again? O boy.

My father was still trying to communicate with us. We would come home and find more glasses broken, the cabinet door wide open.

*You think you woulda been carrying on like this if I was still around? I know ya'll sense me, pick up the little messages I'm leaving. I don't mean to frighten ya'll. You don't know how hard it is to move things. I know you mother talking about getting Father to bless the place. But is still me, y'know, is still me. Everybody right, this thing come like a shock, I wasn't ready for it a tall-tall. But I vex bad girl, to see how is only Boy filling up you mind. I gon keep coming till you see sense. You only sixteen and you education going down the drain. Watch you mother, see how she struggling nuh. She nevah run the whole house before, bills and everything. Is my fault I never prepare things proper. And coping with all four of ya'll. I admire she for turning down the Georgetown offer to take Mary. Is four daughters she got and four daughters it will stay. Now this going away business. I sorry ya'll frighten, that you got to run out the house. I an gon harm ya'll, you know that. Just keep that head on girl. You gon need it where you going.*

I had a party for my sixteenth birthday. I had never had a party before, only the promise of one, a child's party in 1964, when, unbeknown to me there was murder, looting, rape, and the burning down of businesses throughout the country, and my father had called my party off and all I could do was cry.

My good friend Marix helped me to organise this one. Marix was one of those boys who was one day part of the crowd, cycling round the town, going to the cinema and parties, coming up the front steps to lounge on our front porch. Faces came and went but Marix stayed; I don't know if I ever knew his last name, I don't know it now. He was good-natured and dependable, the proverbial shoulder to cry on that every girl needs. It was Marix who had liaised between me and KC, Marix who was the 'cover' when I needed one, Marix who was our escort if Des and I wanted to go to late-night movies. Marix who told me that *he* liked me before *he* did. Marix who lent me his record player, helped with the list of invitees, the sourcing of the 'sounds' (records).

If it wasn't for the fact that my new love was up the river, it would have been the coolest fête in the world. New Amsterdam's party crowd rolled in. JJ, M, Lorna, Glory, the twins, Katie; the Georgetown gang, Hazel, Joey W, my cousins. Old boyfriends even, KC and Micky 'poped'. (gatecrashed) Marix stood at the gate, being a bouncer. But I just missed *him* so bad. Birthday parties, like weddings, had a cake-cutting ceremony. I had to kiss my cousin, who cut the cake with me. Everybody cheered. To hold a 'fête' and have it pass the success goal was a major feat: your place in the popularity league went up triple-fold. But even the congratulatory comments next day at school (*girl dat was a great fête yuh party was the biz girl*) didn't lift my spirits. My sixteenth birthday should have felt special, and it didn't. All I could think about was *him*, the fact that he should have been there, with his arm around me, should have cut the cake with me, should have wowed my friends with his charm, impressed the elders, danced the first dance, placed some small trinket on my wrist to a jealous audience of girlfriends. For what was happening amongst my girlfriends was the splitting into social groups, the pairing off into couples. At the pit of my heart was always the feeling that I was still on the perimeter of whatever was happening.

At the end of February we went down to Georgetown to celebrate our country becoming a Republic. Independence had been granted in 1966, British Guiana had become Guyana. There were episodes we had lived through with our ear to the radio, news of burning buildings and strikes, looting and bombs and murders, recounting of ballot boxes, the reassurances and promises of the three party leaders. We were going through a rite of passage; in our school auditorium we were asked to prepare to unite: the new Guyanese motto was One People, One Nation, One Destiny. There were articles in the school magazine, intelligent debates, exchanges made between the Caribbean islands. We were being made aware that it was time to redress the bloody past we'd inherited. Black girls and boys began to rethink their image, find ways to redeem themselves from being portrayed as victims.

African names replaced given plantation and Christian names, Afro hair became the fashion, Black Power the new mantra.

I attempted a painting of our 'united' peoples which was printed in the school magazine, our six races arranged in a circle. A competition had been held to find a National Anthem. Our Interior became a new link to our identity. Mashramani Festival was created, borrowing an Amerindian name. The *Chronicle* and *Graphic* newspapers carried articles and photographs of the Party leaders, Dr Jagan and his American wife Janet, Dr Burnham, and Peter D'Aguiar. Although all three parties made wholesome speeches about our diverse peoples pulling together to break free from the yoke of colonialism, each party in truth represented its own racial group; in the view of many ordinary Guyanese Jagan was Communist and Indian, Burnham Africanist, D'Aguiar European; those were the foundations on which most people voted.

It's hard to imagine now the power and fear the word 'communism' had held in the sixties.

My parents had shaken their heads as they read the newspaper. This was the era of the Cuban Missile Crisis, President Kennedy, 'Reds Under the Bed'; the Caribbean was America's backyard: with the islands opting for self-rule America didn't want to be caught with her trousers down. Grenada would find that out in a not-too-distant future. Our population was terrified both by our history and the possibility of change.

I had been aware of that word since my primary school days when that pamphlet with the photograph of the burning of Bibles had been branded on my consciousness. All Catholics needed to know about communists was that they were Godless. The Church puffed up its chest. The press portrayed Mrs Jagan as a red anti-American through and through.

Learning about the atom bomb in school, coupled with the reading of American magazines, Catholic theology, and an eclectic reading matter that had progressed from fairy tales through the Famous Five, war comics, Mills & Boon, and British Columbia Outdoors: this was how the reality of the wider world was being brought to me.

Our newly independent Guyana didn't slide smoothly into self-rule. Whilst all the parties voiced a united Guyana, internally they all plotted their own progress and their rivals' downfall. Outside the amphitheatre jaguars were circling: Venezuela was waiting to claim more than a third of Guyana's borders, Suriname was sharpening her teeth along the Corentyne Region.

I cannot remember knowing that, even as we 'celebrated' Republic, in essence another excuse to dress up and party, Guyana's expatriate sons and daughters, famous writers and artists, were in this very Georgetown with other Caribbeans reading poetry, essays, engaging in discussion about the cultural heart of our country. Wilson Harris and Martin Carter, two of Guyana's finest writers, were amongst them. I did not even know their names then, although I could recite practically the whole of Byron's 'Prisoner of Chillon'. The event is not marked in my diary. This is what I write:

February 22nd

*Midnight. Well we're a Republic now. Hear there was some shooting by the borders between Venezuela + Guyana Defence Force. We went to a fête at 1 o'clock Monday morning with 2 guys – Patrick + Joe – Des + I + Hazel had met earlier. Had a groovy time. At 6 o'clock went to the seawall, lovely early in the morning. Patrick was trying to* soor me – anyway it was all kicks and I played hard to get. Those boys are really wicked. Singing 'push it in the girl' all the time. Anyway that's no big thing.

February 23rd

Went to Hazel's mother + spent the day. Joey F, Patrick + Baby Doll were there. Hadda lotta jokes. After lunch went to watch floats. Boys wanted us to go to Pegasus but Mummy, it seemed, had said not to let us go out alone with guys. After all I'm sixteen now. The 2 guys came + stayed till after 11. Hazel's Granny kept sitting there all the time.

February 24th

Desiree + I had to catch the 3 o'clock train and José had brought his car so they dropped us to the station.
When the train had travelled some 10 miles remembered we had left <u>all</u> our make-up! Tough. Mummy + the 2 kids met us at the stelling.
I <u>was</u> surprised.
They never do. Then oh, I nearly fainted with joy and disbelief! He was <u>down</u>! Mummy said he had been at us over the weekend – she said she'd had all the boys!

February 28th

Had quite a day today. There were 2 or 3 last-lap floats that moved today. Berbice Arts Theatre had one. Now I wish I had joined in – it was ELDORA – a golden float. Went tramping till 8 o'clock. Marix joined in later. Moved with JJ then. It was real good but if he had been here, it would have been better.

In March I gave up the cinema for Lent.
Elizabeth raised her eyebrows, remembering years gone by when comics and chocolate had been the sacrifice.
But when I came to her hesitantly, with fear in my mouth and the question in the air, she did not lay down the law.
"It's up to you," she answered this contrary daughter.

Her mind was too full of immigration problems to get involved in another round of arguments.

She could see confusion clouding my face; she knew how disappointed I'd been that 'the boy' hadn't even given me a card for my birthday. Every night I sat looking out the window, my face breaking out like the sun when he appeared, or, as was more likely, sinking into a black sulk of despair. Her warnings were always misconstrued, ended up in slanging matches that 'poor Jim' would turn over and over in his grave if he heard. Not that he didn't. Not a week went by we didn't sense him, smelt those lilies so strongly. Elizabeth had seen him walking up the front steps and she wasn't afraid, but we children were; it was more for our sake than hers that she gathered us up and went to sleep with Jean, or Millie. Sometimes one of the boys slept over, Gordon or Godfrey, Daddy James's grandsons. But that was more for our physical safety than being afraid of a ghost. There were enough bad people out there living ready to cause you harm, rather than those who had departed this earth; some of them as bold as brass climbed right up her front steps with their gold teeth glinting, promising her and her girls the whole world. As for the dead, she lived with more ghosts than her children could ever dream of.

She watched me get ready for the cinema, put on my nice dress, lipstick, smooth my hair with hairspray; pace the gallery for hours until the fact sunk in he wasn't coming. I knew then God was punishing me for breaking my Lenten sacrifice.

He turned up the next night; that seemed to be the pattern – hot, cold, hot, cold – full of charm. My mother did not mince her words. She could see why I was so stupid over him; he was a handsome devil, like one of these Indian movie stars I was always on about, rushing to the Globe on a Saturday afternoon with Katie or Devi. I had even begun to wear a tika on my forehead!

Most of our 'dates', when he turned up, were to the movies. The movies remained everyone's life and blood. We were all film mad. If it wasn't the current Rock Hudson film it was *West Side Story* or Donovan in *If it's Tuesday this must be Belgium*...My diary lists scores of films over that time.

In the Easter holidays he went to work up-river, an echo of my father, but I got dressed up and went to the school fête, danced to the Atlantis band. Willie Gunboat sent Gary to tell me he had had to cool things because I was so young. Did I notice?

My sister sat out on the porch with us now, Marix a constant feature. My mother still told us stories. Spoke to us of her half-sisters Sybil and Ismay, both married and living in Georgetown; how she wished she had a sister close by. She sighed at the memory of the beautiful Lucille. As for her brother...she hadn't had a letter from him for months but now she was considering us going to England.

In May we lost Rio, our Alsatian.

Daddy had bought him as a puppy after they sent my poor Rover up the river. Rio had been treated as more than a yard dog. He ate dog food, not scraps. He was groomed, and taken for proper walks. And then on 6$^{th}$ May we found him dead on the concrete in the front yard. He'd been poisoned.

We all cried as we buried him, and grew afraid. Who would have done a thing like that? And why?

Yet my passion overrode everything, even the daily news reports about the presence of Stokely Carmichael, the Trinidadian Black Power leader on the run in Guyana, the unrest and disturbances.

But with passion had come a routine of dates made and broken, with no apologies and an almost careless disregard for my fledgling feelings. When things were sweet they were sweet as mangoes. I was learning to be a flirt, milking the times when he *did* turn up, when he *was* kissing me, when, like that Sunday afternoon we had to ourselves (where were Mummy and my sisters...cinema? Sunday school?) I let him touch my breasts and stood in front of him on the Berbice chair slowly pulling the zipper on the front of my dress up and down.

At the première of the first West Indian film, *The Right and the Wrong*, he played it cool, his arm hanging loosely over the back of the cinema, watching the beautiful girls in bikinis, and I flushed in the dark, wishing I had *that* body, *those legs*.

His hands started to wander further; evenings on the front porch were frantic: I panicked, caught between desire and fear, my ears perking up during the biology class, trying to decipher information about safe periods *just in case*.

My church attendance had been dropping, slowly but regularly. I disgraced my mother with my penchant for miniskirts and long black leatherette waistcoats à la *Woodstock*. I argued new philosophies with her, about Socialism, America, Russia, and the fact that God was everywhere anyway.

## 20

# Girls Go Wild in Georgetown

*1970*

For years afterwards, whether waiting by the side of a sterile dance floor, or pushing a pram along an English promenade, whether leaning back against the leather of an English pub, or looking out the kitchen window, hands deep in a washing-up bowl, the sight of teenagers would bring those wild August days of 1970 back to me. Never again would the taste of freedom be so sweet nor the sharpening of my personality so assured.

Hazel's front porch, the boys perched there. Afternoons hot and languid, the promise of evening a kaleidoscope slashed across the sky. Myself and Des, hair fresh from curlers, swinging full over our shoulders. The new dog, Spot, nose down on his front paws, already an acknowledged Georgetownian; my kitten Toots too, surviving the ferry crossing and the train down to Georgetown, curled up on my lap. Up the front steps bounded new friends: Harold the young cricketer; Martin the handsome Portuguese artist; Patrick, the tall boy we'd met back at Easter; Dennis, Hazel's cousin; the 'twins' Patrick and Roy.

We had seen Elizabeth off at the airport, waved goodbye to our bewildered younger sisters who were headed overland through Mackenzie for the Kwakwani bush, and us two Berbice girls headed back to Georgetown, prepared to lime.

We weren't concerned with politicians and their business, choke and rob and their business, trade unions and sugar workers and their business, nor with plotters planning to blow up businesses business. We poured Pepsi-Cola for Martin and flirted in our hipster jeans.

Christmas had come in August. From back-of-beyond New Amsterdam which you could cycle round in half an hour, streets you knew like the shape of your lips and busybodies who knew your business more than you, to this grown up sophisticated town: you could spend a day cruising from Vlisssingen Road past the Botanic Gardens, Campbellville, Kitty, the seawall, Kingston; past town houses and the housing scheme, yards and allotments, poor people house, rich people house, Alsatians roaming like wolves inside the perimeters. We got the whistles and the looks; cycle predators cruised up alongside – *where y'all going, Beautiful?* – motorbikes and pillion slowed down, made kissing noises, speeded up. The sun burnt our skin. Our sunglasses came into their own.

And the fêtes! Lord, the fêtes!

It helped that Joey, Hazel's brother, was in a band. And not just any band. One of Guyana's top bands, The Graduates, whose cover tunes and instrumentals, pop hits and jump-up numbers had bodies grinding and wining, getting down and hugging up, giving boys the chance to grind their hips against gleaming midriffs in their hipster pants, slide their spider fingers into the peepholes of dresses.

To know a Boy in a Band was the equivalent of Heaven; you were a highly-evolved angel in this new fast-paced Kingdom of Rhythm. It granted you free entrance to fêtes, barbecues, dinner dances, earned you the ease of cooldom, the title of Liming Princess; you became the recipient of other girls' envy; you learnt the language of interplay of new worlds in full migration through travel, music and fashion. Even skinny bones me felt hot. There was something about Georgetown air that made me tingle. Back when I was eleven it had only made me tremble. But now it felt like a rebirth; my limbs moved with an ease and a languor the Georgetown heat and Demerara breeze poured into my bones.

God knows what old Daddy J would say if he saw this incarnation slide her hot ass on the melting leather seat of some boy's motorbike. Check the long blonde hair and the blue eyes black-ringed with mascara, the pink lipstick lounging on the full lips, the toss of the head, the sunshades. And the hot mouth! Sure now is coming true all those devil child descriptions, and no more are the words hiding at the back of her throat, but snake out sharp and hissing, or smooth and street smart when it suits.

Even Desiree, St Angela herself, change her personality

when she hit town. Dark hair luscious like some señorita, she lolled on Hazel's veranda in shorts, more voluptuous than me, bronze skin and the most beautiful eyes every damn fool commented on. Georgetown didn't know what hit them. Martin the artist, with a ripe age of twenty-three, gravitated towards this fourteen-year-old like a wasp at a picnic.

We cruised downtown where music shops belted out new reggae sounds from Jamaica, and boys spilled out on the pavement, attention split between the sounds and the girls' miniskirts waving like bunting. Young people business was this: having the paisa (or the green or the bread) to buy the latest 45, for music was the business that mek the fête...The whole week was concerned with where was the fête happ'ning *this* weekend man, and who had the sounds to pull it off? Somebody had to be just off the plane with hot discs from the States or Limeyland or now Jamaica or Trini or Barbados where the rumour was Simon and Garfunkel were recording.

Calypso and The Merrymen was for the old people. Now rock steady and reggae and wickedness words come flying in faster than a sneeze. *Lie down girl lemme push it up push it up lie down...*

Judge Dread, Jimmy Cliff, The Jackson Five, The Wailers...boys' voices close to your ear, mouthing the lyrics as you wined your hipbone into their groin.

I could almost hear my grandfather ranting from his Kwakwani pulpit: *You see what I tell you! Devil music taking over the world! I tell you ban the blasted radio!*

And all over the country, parents' voices: *And now they want record? Is how much times you can listen to the same thing? Is addle they brain gon addle, as The Lord is my witness.*


Right from the start us girls were causing commotion. Rumour had it Harold had been 'seeing' some woman in the yard at Kitty; an older woman at that – she was thirty-two! His eye lit on the new talent, and on me, and before spit could dry on hot concrete he was lounging on the porch to the wrath of the somebody in the upstairs flat, who labelled Des and me right away as 'wild girls'.

I got so vex! I hustle, write in Book about the dry-up rass, old woman jealousy and how she dare, how she dare wash her mouth on *me*, trying to ruin my reputation before it even start! Luckily Hazel was moving, and ensconced at Duncan Street, the lime was hot. Even Lorna, herself visiting family for the holidays, came calling, and she and I, shameless, walked barefoot across the city, dressed in bell-bottom trousers.

Of course you still had to do the same stupidness, never mind Mummy wasn't there – you still had to be polite and offer to wash dishes and make up your bed and sweep downstairs yard and help hang out clothes and all that rubbish. But done when it done, off on the bicycles and gone, from Lamaha Street then the world.

This Georgetown wasn't the Georgetown that I remembered from my St Rose's days, when I was on the outside looking in, a nobody.

This wasn't the Georgetown Des and I knew from children days either. Hey. No.

You're out there baby, you and Des, sweet country blood for the thin Georgetown mosquitoes. It was almost like the movies: the stores, the wide streets, the gears, cloze man hot cloze, nice looking boys, smart-smart girls with their nose up in the air...

*You daddy dead so you can lime.*

We went to the cinema as often as we had in New Amsterdam, and always in a group. Harold was openly sooring me, and I was in a flummox as to how I could still deep down love my man so bad and yet get so excited by handsome boys, motorbikes, boys with soul, boys who could banter and parlay...well the choice was just too much. I went to the movies with Harold once, and enjoyed his kisses as much as I enjoyed a fudgicle, though it was fight I had to fight his hand away from the hemline of my skirt.

I confessed all to Book, and would later even tell *him* how yes, when I was in town you know, *all that time and you never wrote me once, you never came to see me once, but cheups man, you know plenty boys was tracking me you know and I let one kiss me, yes sir.*

And things didn't stop there...

What is it about old people that they have to ruin young people fun?

Hazel's Granny was the fly in the ointment, the downpour on the beach, the marabunta at the picnic. Washed her mouth on us New Amsterdam girls, at the frequency with which the boys, including her own grandsons, climbed up her grand-daughter's front porch. From the first day she had berated me for not showering both morning and night, cranking me up so much I dropped my pretend good behaviour at being in someone else's house and brought all my home-ways into being: argued, sulked, stropped, ignored, was rude, wilful and moody, and in Book, 'went to town':

*I have never been so disgraced + this will not rest. The comments continued. D + I spoke to Hazel about it. H said she didn't see anything wrong with 1 or 2 guys coming. But neither Des nor I had asked the other two – one which I'd never seen before anyway.*
[Memories of Cookie surfaced] *Mistress Harris, this one has got a plaster for every sore.*

There was another band playing the kind of music I was growing to like. A touch of Santana, Hendrix...The bongo player's name was Michael. I don't know what it was about him that drew me. They were playing outdoors on a hot tropical night infused by the scent of roses and gingerliles, barbecue grill, cigarette smoke, the mint breath of newly showered boys and us girls wearing our mothers' scents as closely as our halter tops. Boys circled like cheetahs: Guyanese, Canadians, Americans, the clipped accent of the English. There were no parents to cramp your style. The music played by young men who used guitars as extensions of their sexuality...which girl would not find herself drawn to the bongo player? He was playing heartbeats, he was playing pulse, he was tuning our rhythm, feeding the dance which lit up our body like a fuse. The cheetahs lost lustre, became hummingbirds dipping into a profusion of lipsticked mouths. The beating heart of the bongo connected with everybody on that decking, laid down for dancing on lawn. And connected with me in a way that would find recognition decades later when I stumbled across the music of Salif Keita, and when I learnt to play the djembe. But at that time it connected viscerally, a strange and immediate attraction communicating itself through the eyes.

Michael just happened to be Hazel's landlord's son. He just happened to be a friend of Joey's. He just happened to call round the next day and join the boys on the porch, only staying long enough to make a date for the Astor. And in the cinema he would turn to me and say "Don't wear see-thru when you're with me," and although his arm burnt my shoulder through the film, he held himself back, not offering or inviting any intimacy. Even when we said goodbye a couple of days later, with Des and me getting ready to return to NA, and me being pathetically dramatic by wearing black, he didn't reach out to me. Instead he said he didn't know why he hadn't kissed me in the cinema, didn't know why he'd come to see me and even though he wanted to kiss me didn't think that Hazel's front porch was the time and the place. All nonsense I guess, thinking it through now, and remembering the one letter I received, and the hint of suppressed passion, warning me he was dangerous, and how I hung on for weeks waiting for another which never came and how turned on I was even though my loverman was still in my veins.

And that was it, that summer, gone in short remembrances of peppermint kisses, the sharp aftershave of boys, cruising by the seawall, being conscious of the power of being a girl, music like a drug in the blood. Smell and heat and skin, fingertips on elbows, movements like salamanders across hot sand. At the far reaches of my memory I would recall faster, wilder boys at fêtes, talking about drugs, something called MX, but I couldn't even contemplate the need for anything more hallucinogenic than those August holidays had been.

# 21

# Verandas

How many young women have waited on porches and verandas like these? Some nights you can hear the drums. Steady like heartbeats they come over fences, from backyards surrounded by galvanize, beneath a variable moon. Behind this façade of civilization there are those who pass small parcels of blood and dirt, locks of hair, snippets of fingernails. The stories we hear implant themselves deep into our souls. Even as we say the Angelus I know that Fairmaids are walking up from their river, their hair smelling of the sea, their smile ready for the young man waiting at the gate. Here in this land of the bacoo, of ole higues, of Kanaima, the water mamma is as real as this flat nose on my face. I see her in the swish of skirts in the market place, the knowingness in which they watch me, say to my mother *you have a right one here.* What can they see that I don't know? My unconscious thoughts, of kisses and dreams, sweet music and sheets of white paper to scrawl on may all have meaning I have no control over. In this skin I am not responsible for, I walk, in the shadow of those who have gone before me, heading for some light that constantly changes in intensity. *Jesus, the Light of the world*, they said. But are they all wrong, those others – those goddesses smiling down from Devi's altar, the woman by the river in the red headtie, my Uncle Reggie and his mystic books, my own Grandmother Angie?

I want to be a sorceress, why was I not born with the caul?

*There is more to sight than seeing.*
O Book! Book! Thank God I have you. I will always have you. I will always have you.

16th

*If he had not come tonight, I would not have given in so easily. He came in the midst of my doubt and the pendulum is* swinging again. He says he loves me, he says he is sorry for what happened on Sunday night. He asked me to forget all he said then. But I cannot forget. I cannot forget the pain I felt on Monday and Tuesday. I lied when I told him that as he had come back it would be harder for me to leave him. Yes I lied. For I know that if he hurt me the way he did on Sunday night, I will easily forget him. I cannot analyse my feelings at this moment. All I know is what could have been a beautiful relationship has been spoilt. For in future I shall never trust someone as much as I have him. I shall never depend on someone as much. I shall never give as much of myself – as I have given to my first love. And now in my undecided state I shall let things drift. When he told me he would never do what he did on Sunday nite again etc etc I hushed him up and said, make no more promises, let us only live for now.*

Oh God! If my mother knew what I was getting up to on the front porch!

Seventeen years old and nothing but heat. Heat in the sweat that poured down this new traitorous body. Heat that didn't stir in the wake of the breeze of the paper fan, folded from carefully torn-out pages of my exercise book. Heat in the drowsiness of my eyelids as I droop over my desk in class; in the pulse at my temple that throbbed at the memory of his kisses the night before, at the love-bite on my neck I had tried to disguise with foundation...Heat on the long bike ride home from school, the marabuntas slow under the house, the dog's yawn, the cat's half-opened eyes on the step. Heat on my fingertips and scorched in the palm of my hand where he had forced me to touch him. Forced me, my God. Dragged my protesting fingers with the pink nails that had been quite content to play with the edges of his hair, walk across his chin, his neck, circle his shirt button, opening it, all the time looking him straight in the eye brazen like those starlets on the movies. We'd been on the front porch gone nine o'clock, the street dark, house lights going out and no movement or sound apart from his breath on my neck and a flitter of fireflies. After a stream of kisses he'd manoeuvred me up on the porch rail, his voice hoarse as he said *don't worry I won't let you go* as I got frightened of falling into the yard below. Three, four weeks now of movies, sitting at the back of Balcony. Thank Christ it was so dark and Clark Gable and Marilyn Monroe were keeping everybody's ears and eyes occupied. I betrayed myself by moving nearer and nearer and not being able to breathe, like I was waiting for him to kill me right there with his mouth at my throat. The sudden image of Elizabeth calling me a whore and the nuns chastising me with their tongues and the cane *fast sinful wild nasty Jezebel* terrified me more and I managed to drag his hand off, and sit up and move along the seat. He wouldn't speak to me then. Walked out of the cinema leaving me bruised, inside and out.

*Don't tease me, you bitch.*

In the daytime, watching Mary play with her dolls, I asked myself howcome only yesterday I was playing too, consumed by moving the dolls' plastic arms and legs about, positioning them on chairs we'd made ourselves out of match boxes, consumed by cutting out and hand-sewing miniature evening dresses and skirts, dressing them to kill. Now all I thought about was *his* mouth, the way he leaned on the porch with his brown eyes watching, a cigarette burning down between his fingers. I waited, on fire.

And then last night. Under a new moon he'd kissed and kissed me till my lips hurt.

*Have you ever...?* He'd whispered. God, how embarrassing. I was thankful for the darkness, flushed at his use of the word, that word I'd only just come across in a book one of my girlfriends had lent me. He'd leaned back and laughed. He had had experience of course, and could laugh. *You know,* he'd said, *women have them too.* But I wouldn't answer him, didn't dare tell him about that passage in Lady Chatterley which was being passed round the class, and that when it was my turn to take it home I'd read it under the sheet with a torch...

I couldn't, wouldn't say any of this, and all of a sudden he discarded the cigarette he'd lit, his eyes becoming as muddy as the yard, and reached for me on the dark porch as my mother and sisters slept behind closed doors. He bared my neck and throat, making necklaces with his teeth and tongue, swung me up to sit on the rail, whispering *don't fight don't fight don't you want to know what it's like?* Beat my protesting hands away like annoying birds, then trapped them, holding them fast. My whole body was caught between the grip of wanting and not wanting, a chrysalis fluttering away waiting to break out. Then his bare skin for the first time; his hands moulding me between flesh and bone, muscle and blood, my hands breaking free to hold on to the rail, neck upturned to the fall of his mouth breaking into the night. Things are different in daytime. The porch basks in sunlight and watches the interplay between two young lovers who know their time is limited and don't know how to behave. We fight for dignity and self-possession. Play-fighting and teasing turns to anger as he rips up my Hare Krishna card. He slaps me and heads for Betty's Bar.

Indoors, plans are being made, discussions circling between the possibility of migrating to Canada or the UK.

Love for rivermen holds fast through long absences after the tide bears them away. Holds fast through the smoulder from their dark eyes. On his return the riverman needs to reground, re-root, shake the river from his boots. There are spaces near the river where clothes dry and fingers walk over skin.

*Soon it will be my turn to go but I gon come back and marry you,* the country girl says. She is poised above him. She can hear the river sloshing up on the bank, feel the roughness of coconut matting on her knees. She ignores it. There were new things to discover; the firelight in his eyes when she did something he liked, the vulnerability of his flesh, the liquid that ran between them...so this is why love and passion in this country was wild and undisciplined, broke all the barriers of religion and legal marriage.

*I will have a daughter for you,* she dreamed, *and name her Cyane Farida. We shall be married in both our religions.*

"I don't want to go to England," he says. "I don't like that place. Why don't you wait, and we'll go to the States."

# 22

# Where Poems Came

Hot mouth girl, enough. This is how I prefer to remember...which from the age of eleven poor Book tried to transcribe...That room of childhood where the rain is beating on the window pane and you are curled up on the Berbice chair reading...At the outer edge of your vision your sisters undress the cold American dolls, love them and chastise them in turn...The book you are reading is of other worlds far, far removed from this one...

*Why you so rude? Why you so hardears?* Three slaps with a palm, a lash with a belt. *No I don't want to leave Anne of Green Gables and lay the table.* Desiree smiles her grey-eyed smile and passes Mummy the diaper pins.

At Christmas because you have the hair you are Gabriel: *You, Maiden, are with child...*Mary is Mary; Des, Joseph; Yonnette the Baby Jesus.

Your daddy plucks the strings of his Hawaiian guitar, lifts the conch to his lips. The neighbours gather round the front steps listening, just like in those Elvis films. The strings drop into eternity. *Mary's Boy Child* and *Jingle Bells* spills from the radio. That radio, the new storyteller...Wearing his conch shell crown, he brings you *The Little White Bull, The Everly Brothers, Lata Mangeshka, José Feliciano, Tom Dooley, Tell Laura I Love Her, Frenchman's Creek...*side by side with those stories they tell when rain is falling, when the night draws in; jumbie stories that have you too frightened to go down the passageway for a glass of water for the storyteller's throat.

Every scratch of the dounze tree against the back porch sends you screaming. These tales are alive and breathing; they are not confined within the safety of pages accompanied by slumbering, beautiful paintings of European women and wizards, castles and swans.

No, these are real stories, told by that person sitting there in front of you in words that are not burdened by the weight of grammar but are punctuated by sigh and tone, laughter and pauses fed by the listeners themselves, waiting with bated breath and questions hanging off a lip or burdened by the weight of their own tongues. Go to bed with fear or a tune on your lips, wake up with it sitting there. Then, seek any bit of paper you can find, a used envelope, the pages of exercise books, copy lyrics from the radio...

The words are left naked on the page, bare without their music, comfortless without their vocalist. But in their tragedy they are beautiful, like Aunty Jean's dressmaker's model they are waiting to *become*. See the way the end words rhyme, the way a narrative unfolds. See how repetition works, the chorus bringing you back to the centre, causing you to pre-empt its rhythm. Fear is held between breaths; between beats your breath, like the listener, waits.

So poems are born.

Read on the front porch before the sun goes down, or by the light of the kerosene lamp. Read anything, the *National Geographic* magazine Aunt Lucille Mittelholzer gave you, a passage from the Psalms, a sonnet from Shakespeare. Lord Byron, *The Prisoner of Chillon. Macbeth, Macbeth, Margarette. The Highwayman.*

So Daddy might have read to Mama as she died slowly in that St John Street bedroom sharing images of other worlds apart from those she'd known – the silence of the Berbice River, a canoe sliding soundlessly up a sandbank, sandflies and mosquitoes, a mother telling her of someone called Massa...his voice and the radio would have told her the story of New Amsterdam, its newly paved streets and wooden houses, American salesmen and Avon ladies... Her ears would have heard the town grow, from cartwheels rolling on that pot-holed road to bicycle bells and the postman calling, Betty with her *Feesh!* clambering up the backsteps, the spluttering of motorbikes, the glide of cars, the news of workers flinging bottle bombs into department stores, the promises of politicians punctuating the airwaves, Death Announcements solemnly read out, the bells of all the churches ringing, Pentecostals gospelling, grandchildren swinging on the iron gates, Bing Crosby and Elvis, The Beatles.

The rustling of the coconut palms would have come through the bedroom window, the smell of rain, the chattering of kiskadees.

And even as I recite some poem at the age of ten to the Anglican priest in our living room, on the eve of his return to England, even then the world was turning, and turning, and turning.

And poems are born of love of course, and loss, and death. And the rhythm of the Caribbean bursting through every waking morning, each twilight. So poems are born.

And so I go, with Daddy's guitar which the air hostess places carefully in the baggage hold above my head.

"Do you play?" she asks.

"No, no," I say, as I would again and again, regretting.

And so I go, after all those months of planning. The art school in Toronto didn't happen, Britain did, Cyril Hawker's land.

Despite my tragic love affair, I was young, I was excited. I was looking forward to my new life as an artist.

I didn't know then of the things I would miss…

Our school prom at the Town Hall, white dresses and corsages. Sunshine. Curry and roti. Star-apples. The smell of my grandmother, the feel of her silvering hair as we brushed it down her back. My grandfather's glowering looks. The little green rocking chair. Our front porch, the sound of bicycle bells. The crash of a coconut in the yard. Saturday morning at the market, wet fish on ice, the river. Sunday mass, the chatter at the church door, the smell of incense, church hats and organdie dresses.

My New Amsterdam, its streets, shops, houses, the Round the Town bus, the country buses with the world on the roof, and hope in those names along the side. Saturday matinées, Indian films. My sisters tumbling round the house. Bike rides up the stelling. My friends, my friends, my best friend Lorna…the hailing of someone who knows you.

There are other things I will miss – the pain on my mother's face, the waiting for a buyer for the house. Borrowing money to survive. The Burnham years.

But even more important, the opportunity to be part of a country who was growing up at the same time as me, stepping out from the control of her rulers. The whole process is bloody and painful. Despite all her tragedy, I miss the intimate knowing of her, the stories that had not yet fallen from my father's lips, the chain of ancestry that was broken. How close I would sit on his knee and ask him now, about Fort Nassau, about the river, about the birds and fish, the names of plants, the traces of Africa, South America, Barbados, Europe. I do not know whether he was descended from a free man or a slave; there were a people called the Kru, boatmen from Africa who came as free men in the nineteenth century. Could James Alexander Harris Senior have been one of these?

I would turn to my grandmother too, and ask her about Evelyn, about Rosa, about Madeira, about Fairmaids.

And you my love, I know now, will always be a metaphor for my country.

So many of us have gone now, Mother and Daddy James, Aunt Ena, Uncle Beau, Wallace and Doodoo, Uncle Compton, Dennis...Dispersed in cemeteries from New Amsterdam to Georgetown.

And my friends, scattered like stars across the ocean...Elly and I renewed our friendship in the UK. Lorna writes from the US. Devi and I recently discovered each other on the Net. Barbara and I are in touch.

I would return once more to Guyana, in 1978, to a country that had changed completely. I would see my lover just that once more, and wave goodbye to him from the *Torani* steamer across the Berbice River to the strains of the Stones' *This will be the Last Time...*

There is a bridge now, across the Berbice River.

I would be artist, factory worker, wife, mother, writer...

I am blessed to have my mother still; without her this book would not have been written. Names fade into the mist. Brazh, Machado, Hawker. My mind spins as I trawl genealogy websites; there are thousands of us there, all trying to reconnect, all plotting those thousands of silver trails across the Atlantic.

And this last I hold in my imagination, and pass to my children and grandchildren: as I think of my plane lifting into the sky on August 1$^{st}$, 1971, heading for open sea, I look below and see them – all our mothers and fathers, and they are looking up at me from beneath white canvas sails, heading for Guiana, the land of many waters, hands at their brows as the dazzling sun hits the fuselage on the wing of my aeroplane.

▪ The author's grandfather, "Daddy J", and Portuguese grandmother, Angela. They brought up the author's mother Elizabeth as their own, following the early death of Elizabeth's birth mother Evelyn, Angela's sister. The author's by-blood grandfather was a white second generation Scottish immigrant, Cyril. He died soon after his wife, Evelyn.